A Leadership Playbook for Addressing Rapid Change in Education

A Leadership Playbook for Addressing Rapid Change in Education provides educational leaders with a simple, step-by-step approach for addressing rapid change. Drawing on the model of appreciative inquiry, this book provides detailed examples of educational problems and provides the who, what, where, when, why, and how to achieve change. Author Teresa L. San Martín emphasizes the traits of outstanding and exceptional leaders: trust; collaborative efforts; communicating with empathy and care. Detailed play-by-play examples are provided that show how school administrators are able to solve relevant problems of practice such as how to create productive and focused high school teacher teams, how educational leaders can increase teacher retention, and how district administrators can provide innovative and meaningful staff development opportunities. This timely book—which supports educators as they continue to grapple with the effects of the pandemic—provides real solutions, equipping school administrators with the tools necessary to confront perpetual change occurring in today's complex educational environment.

Teresa L. San Martín is a former teacher, elementary building administrator, and district level assistant superintendent. She teaches online courses at the graduate level, modeling and applying appreciative inquiry with students or when volunteering in the community.

T0383600

Other Eye On Education Books Available from Routledge

(www.routledge.com/eyeoneducation)

Mismeasuring Schools' Vital Signs
Steve Rees and Jill Wynns

First Aid for Teacher Burnout:
How You Can Find Peace and Success, 2nd Edition
Jenny Grant Rankin

Leading School Culture through Teacher Voice and Agency
Sally J. Zepeda, Philip D. Lanoue, David R. Shafer, Grant M. Rivera

Becoming an International School Educator:
Stories, Tips, and Insights from Teachers and Leaders
Edited by Dana Specker Watts and Jayson W. Richardson

The Principal's Desk Reference to Professional Standards:
Actionable Strategies for Your Practice
Robyn Conrad Hansen and Frank D. Davidson

Trailblazers for Whole School Sustainability:
Case Studies of Educators in Action
Cynthia L. Merse, Jennifer Seydel, Lisa A.W. Kensler, and David Sobel

Get Organized Digitally!:
The Educator's Guide to Time Management
Frank Buck

The Confident School Leader:
7 Keys to Influence and Implement Change
Kara Knight

Empowering Teacher Leadership:
Strategies and Systems to Realize Your School's Potential
Jeremy D. Visone

Creating, Grading, and Using Virtual Assessments:
Strategies for Success in the K-12 Classroom
Kate Wolfe Maxlow, Karen L. Sanzo, and James Maxlow

Building Learning Capacity in an Age of Uncertainty:
Leading an Agile and Adaptive School
James A. Bailey

Leadership for Deeper Learning:
Facilitating School Innovation and Transformation
Jayson W. Richardson, Justin Bathon, Scott McLeod

A Leadership Playbook for Addressing Rapid Change in Education

Empowered for Success

Teresa L. San Martín

Routledge
Taylor & Francis Group

NEW YORK AND LONDON

Designed cover image: © Getty Images

First published 2023
by Routledge
605 Third Avenue, New York, NY 10158

and by Routledge
4 Park Square, Milton Park, Abingdon, Oxon, OX14 4RN

Routledge is an imprint of the Taylor & Francis Group, an informa business

Library of Congress Cataloging-in-Publication Data
Names: San Martin, Teresa, author.
Title: A leadership playbook for addressing rapid change in education: empowered for success/Teresa San Martin.
Description: New York, NY: Routledge, 2023. | Includes bibliographical references and index.
Identifiers: LCCN 2022041967 | ISBN 9781032396675 (hardcover) | ISBN 9781032396132 (paperback) | ISBN 9781003350804 (ebook)
Subjects: LCSH: Educational leadership. | Educational change. | Teacher-administrator relationships. | School management and organization.
Classification: LCC LB2806 .S326 2023 | DDC 371.2/011—dc23/eng/20221216
LC record available at https://lccn.loc.gov/2022041967

ISBN: 978-1-032-39667-5 (hbk)
ISBN: 978-1-032-39613-2 (pbk)
ISBN: 978-1-003-35080-4 (ebk)

DOI: 10.4324/9781003350804

Typeset in Palatino
by codeMantra

This book is dedicated to the post-pandemic educational leaders. Change is certain and bringing clarity to a rapid decision-making process is paramount.

Contents

Meet the Author

Teresa L. San Martín began her "official" inquiry journey in 2006 when she enrolled in a doctoral program determined to learn how to appropriately conduct educational research with the goal of helping teachers and administrators struggling with the change process, decision-making, and educational reform efforts. She was determined to find a solutions-based model to help address issues and problems that plagued schools and districts that needed rapid change and response.

At the time she began her research, schools and districts were in the middle of the No Child Left Behind (NCLB) era (under Title 1 of the No Child Left Behind Act of 2001). Schools and districts across the nation were being judged as high performing or failing based on student performance levels in reading and math. In her review of problem-solving change models, she discovered the work of David Cooperrider's 1986 research with a doctor's clinic in Cleveland, OH, where the traditional problem-solving method had been dropped for a more participative, generative, and inclusive approach known as appreciative inquiry.

Since then, she has applied the appreciative inquiry method as the change model for solving problems of practice in education. She helps teachers, administrators, schools, and districts discover a more appreciative way of approaching problems with a positive mindset that accelerates and sustain their growth efforts. She has used the appreciative inquiry approach with K-12 teacher curriculum committees in establishing course standards, curriculum and assessment alignment, and textbook adoptions; with strategic planning efforts at the district level; helping a high school turn around the school's reputation; and helping teacher teams/PLCs learn to be more productive. Her appreciative inquiry work has taken her internationally and nationally, working with non-profit entities and public and private schools/districts.

A graduate of the University of Kansas, she moved to Wichita, KS and taught middle school math and English for 11 years. She continued her education, completing a Master's degree in Educational Administration and Supervision (1988) and a Doctorate degree in Educational Leadership (2008) from Wichita State University. She concluded her 35-year career as a practitioner (teacher, elementary building administrator, and district level assistant superintendent) in 2014. She continues to teach online courses at the graduate level, modeling and applying appreciative inquiry with students or when volunteering in the community.

Teresa and her husband, Lazaro (a retired, career educator and coach, as well), live in "la casita de la playa" 400 feet from the beach in Florida—a dream that became their reality in 2017! They enjoy sunrises, surf fishing, and traveling, which includes a loop throughout the Midwest visiting their three adult children and families!

Preface

A gift

The road to excellence has been peppered with silver bullets full of promises over the past few decades in the United States as educational leaders have searched for ways to make decisions about complex problems that are mandated or need reforming and are often perplexed how to make rapid change efforts happen. The metaphorical, silver bullet promises, full of magical solutions to educational issues, have emerged from all corners of research with many based on best practices of *what works* in schools from instructional strategies (Marzano et al., 2001) and classroom management (Marzano et al., 2003) to student positive behavior interventions and supports (Lane et al., 2009) with participation in school wide efforts like response-to-intervention reform (Gresham, 2002) and school turnaround models (Kutash et al., 2010). Schools have been and continue to be in a state of constant flux.

Experts have defined the school as needing to be a learning organization and community (Senge, 2006; Sergiovanni, 1992). The birth of a school learning community (Kruse et al., 1994) and professional learning communities (DuFour & Eaker, 1998; Hord, 1997) became popular tools for school reform. Change and reform efforts continued when leadership standards were established in 1996 defining expectations and practices for school administrators who in turn would promote higher levels of student achievement. Effective leadership standards have undergone revisions as the roles and responsibilities in schools have changed (National Policy Board for Educational Administration, 2015).

Educational leaders discovered during the No Child Left Behind Act of 2001 era, which continued with Every Student Succeeds Act enacted in 2015, the characteristics of successful, high poverty schools (Barone, 2006), and became well versed on the qualities of effective teachers (Stronge, 2007; Whitaker, 2013) and traits of high performing school teams (Marzano et al., 2016). Educational leaders touted their knowledge, reciting Blankstein's (2004) six principles that guided student achievement in high performing schools and were able to revisit what constituted an effective school (Lezotte & McKee Snyder, 2011) while struggling to find ways to meet adequate yearly progress, avoiding the label of a school in need of improvement or failing.

As educational leaders across the nation were being groomed to meet educational challenges and to foster academic success as delineated in the

Interstate School Leaders Licensure Consortium (ISLLC) standards, the pendulum began to swing in another direction when 48 of the 50 states developed a standardized set of common standards determining what students should know and be able to do by the time they graduated from high school. The college and career ready, common core state standards were developed in the areas of English/language arts and math in 2009 to ensure that all students could receive a world class education and be equipped with the skills to compete globally (Common Core State Standards Initiative, 2021).

Educational problems of practice then became twofold, how to provide effective professional development in the areas of college and career ready common core state standards while simultaneously acquiring the technology skills needed to support learning and teaching in a wireless, mobile world where 1:1 laptop, ipad computing, and bring your own device (BYOD) initiatives along with high stakes, technology-enabled state assessments were quickly becoming the norm during the early 2000s (Neuenswander, 2015).

Educational leaders experimented with new adult learning experiences determining what worked with ongoing, job embedded staff development (Guskey & Yoon, 2009; Zepeda, 2011). On the job training or job embedded staff development was intended to provide meaningful adult learning experiences in real time with immediate feedback via instructional coaches, peer coaching, mentoring, video recordings, and lesson study where planning, funding, time, and trust were and continue to be major factors in teacher development (Zepeda, 2019).

The technology explosion had exponentially discombobulated any sense of educational normalcy. Educators jumped on the technology train embracing a digital approach to learning that has helped create a more student-centered environment with mobile devices creating an opportunity for renewal and reform. Best practices pertaining to technology integration (Pitler et al., 2012), adoption of technology tools and access to, and technology-related staff development have consumed the energy of educational leaders as financial decision-making and solutions impacted educational leaders (Digital Promise, 2014) during the first two decades of the 21st century. Educators had been experimenting with the role technology could take to support instruction, first with laptop initiatives, then the introduction of the ipad, Chromebooks, and smartphones.

The educational school year came to an abrupt halt in 2020 due to the Covid-19 pandemic, which forced school closures. To minimize educational disruption, pedagogically skilled teachers PreK through higher educational institutions found themselves ill-equipped with the sudden shift to the blended/hybrid and fully online/remote learning models as the new norm for educational delivery. Educators experienced more technology-driven change and chaos during 2020, than in the past 40 years when the first microcomputers appeared in classrooms. The unprecedented impact technology has made on the educational system can be construed as an opportunity to help build capacity of educational leaders including both teachers and administrators in understanding what works in terms of instructional efficiency and which modes of educational delivery work best for certain student populations. The constant activity and dramatically accelerating pace of change in the school as a learning organization will likely continue to impact the school's culture, as well as the urgency for interactions and solutions of those involved.

Change has become perpetual motion for educational leaders, and decision-making is essential, but they do not have to be the result of negatively motivated reactions, nor a stab at another hopeful silver bullet solution. How do educational leaders address the challenges and solve the problems they encounter? They approach the problems and uncertainties by trying different approaches, applying research-based practices to their own settings, thinking creatively, designing, implementing new ideas, and reflecting on the effectiveness of their decisions. Employing design thinking is a collaborative effort as educational leaders search for solutions to improve processes and reach desired outcomes. Henriksen and Richardson (2017) see design thinking as "a strategic approach to analyzing and finding solutions to messy real-world problems" (p. 61).

A Leadership Playbook for Addressing Rapid Change in Education: Empowered for Success presents a specific design thinking model that will help educational leaders become more empowered to explore and create a positive, efficient, and effective roadmap or game plan when encountering issues and problems of educational practice. The AI change model as the design thinking approach has been proven worldwide in varied business and non-profit venues.

Through the AI change model, you, as the change leader, and those you work with on a day-to-day basis are in control of what happens—you control the future, your destiny. You will discover that the power is within you as the change leader and those you collaborate with in your administrative team. Success is based on the choices and actions taken collectively as you work through the steps in the AI change model to find what works for you, your schools, the district, and community. AI, as the choice for a rapid change model, is a systemic approach that provides a solutions-based, guiding framework for decision-making that helps you address complex problems and issues in education. It is important that you and your administrative team have a *go-to* change model process to address the issues and problems in educational practices; even more so, being familiar with a design thinking, change model like AI provides "a way to intentionally work through getting stuck" (Watson, 2015, p. 16).

The process of using a non-hierarchical, decision-making model to facilitate change with a positive, participatory model was borrowed from the business world and is known as AI with its 4-D cycle. This book is specifically written for educational leaders seeking *how* to facilitate rapid, sustainable change using a worldwide proven decision-making model. The purpose of the book, *A Leadership Playbook for Addressing Rapid Change in Education: Empowered for Success*, is to provide educational leaders with a decision-making tool involving a collaborative, optimistic approach for facilitating real change and realizing school success immediately with relevant and authentic play-by-play examples. This book is offered as both a philosophy, or way of thinking, and a rapid, step-by-step change process that is solutions-based, uses a positive mindset, and helps educational leaders bring clarity to the decision-making process in a fast-paced environment where change can immediately make an impact.

The word, empowered, in the title means that you are accepting a gift—a license, the official authority, the okay. Success then is defined as a favorable or desired outcome—an accomplishment or achievement. I think of success as a point in time. Success is an event that accomplishes its intended purpose. Therefore, *A Leadership Playbook for Addressing Rapid Change in Education: Empowered for Success* is an essential go-to book, focused on *how* to facilitate success, and grants you the official permission and authority to participate in a process where you learn how to create your future—your destiny as an educational leader.

The following chapters will walk you through the steps so you can learn how to facilitate change, expediting the decision-making process. Whether you are an educational leader at the district or building level, you can implement the AI rapid, change model. A district level administrator can facilitate the change process with a large sector of the school community involving hundreds of participants or a building principal can help facilitate teacher teams or the entire staff in becoming more productive, moving toward consensus decision-making. *A Leadership Playbook for Addressing Rapid Change in Education: Empowered for Success* will be invaluable as you confront problems of practice and undertake change initiatives in your school or district.

How this book is organized

This book is designed to help educators learn how one of the world's most premier decision-making methods is used to arrive at solutions and bring about rapid, sustainable change. Educational leaders are constantly confronted with questions whether at the district level or school level: "How can we...."? (e.g., How can we address student's loss of learning during the pandemic? How can we develop a strong and accountable district leadership team? How can we help teachers build a supporting classroom environment where students can develop social and emotional learning skills?). The answers to your questions—the possibilities and solutions exist within the teams you work with whether you are leading your school or district. The book is divided into two parts. Part I answers the *Who, What, Why, and How* to the AI process, and Part II provides scenarios with play-by-play steps based on the author's experiences using the AI change model detailing the *Where, When,* and *How*.

Part I, Chapters 1–4

The first part of the book is organized to help you understand the *Who, What, Why,* and *How* to use the change model known as AI with four steps in the cycle: Discovery, Dream, Design, and Destiny. Chapters 1 and 2 help you become familiar with *what* AI is as a change model, *why* AI and the four-step (4-Ds) process works, and how AI can help you be successful with change and decision-making frequently encountered within your school or district. Chapter 2 also shares *who* uses the change model and *why* they chose the change method known as the AI 4-D cycle versus other more traditional problem-solving models. Chapters 3 and 4 provide the *how* to use AI as the preferred method or strategy for change and decision-making.

Part II, Chapters 5–9

The second part of the book consists of Chapters 5–9. Scenarios, as stories with a purpose, are detailed to help you more fully understand the *where* and *when* to use the AI 4-D cycle change model and *how* to apply the decision-making process to your educational setting so you can lead fast-paced change in your school or district. The design purpose for the chapters in Part II is written in a playbook format, a step-by-step plan, where each chapter provides a different, applicable scenario, a story with purpose. Each scenario addresses an educational issue or challenge (problem of practice) that becomes the topic of inquiry or focus using the change model known as the AI with its 4-D cycle. The scenarios are based on the author's more than ten years of educational experience when in the positions as a district-wide assistant superintendent or building level administrator.

She used the AI 4-D cycle as the preferred design thinking method to help bring about rapid change in public and private schools and non-profits, across the nation and internationally. School administrators, teachers, and community members were actively engaged in the AI 4-D change process with the examples provided, along with selected responses and action planning solutions. This is a distillation of the author's work with multiple schools and school districts. The examples come from their work.

The chapter format for each scenario is the same throughout Part II. Some scenarios occur at the school building level and others at the school district level. A review of each scenario provides deeper understanding how AI can be used as the preferred change method for making rapid decisions and implementation plans; participant numbers vary in each scenario and range from several to more than 150 people. Chapter 9 begins with a list of potential topics for inquiry that you may be contemplating. The chapter leaves a guided workspace and opportunity to create your own step-by-step plan or playbook, so you too can work toward a solution for the leadership teams you work with in your school or district.

References

Barone, D. M. (2006). *Narrowing the literacy gap: What works in high-poverty schools*. The Guilford Press.

Blankstein, A. M. (2004). *Failure is not an option™: Six principles that guide student achievement in high-performing schools*. Corwin.

Common Core State Standards Initiative. (2021). *Development process*. Common Core State Standards Initiative. http://www.corestandards.org/-about-the-standards/development-process/

Digital Promise. (2014, November 13). *Improving ed-tech purchasing*. Digital Promise: Accelerating Innovation in Education. Education Industry Association. https://digitalpromise.org/2014/11/13/improving-ed-tech-purchasing/

DuFour, R., & Eaker, R. (1998). *Professional learning communities at work: Best practices for enhancing student achievement*. Solution Tree.

Every Student Succeeds Act (ESSA), 20 U.S.C. § 6301 (2015). https://www.congress.gov/114/plaws/publ95/PLAW-114publ95.pdf

Gresham, F. M. (2002). Responsiveness to intervention: An alternative approach to learning disabilities. In R. Bradley, L. Danielson, & D. Hallahan (Eds.), *Identification of learning disabilities: Research to practice* (pp. 242–258). Erlbaum.

Guskey, T. R., & Yoon, K.S. (2009). What works in professional development? *Phi Delta Kappan, 90*(7), 495–500. http://outlier.uchicago.edu/computerscience/OS4CS/landscapestudy/resources/Guskey-and-Yoon-2009.pdf

Henriksen, D., & Richardson, C. (2017). Teachers are designers: Addressing problems of practice in education. *Phi Delta Kappan, 99*(2), 60–64. https://doiorg.ezproxy.fhsu.edu/10.1177/0031721717734192

Hord, S. M. (1997). *Professional learning communities: Communities of continuous inquiry and improvement.* Southwest Educational Developmental Laboratory. https://sedl.org/pubs/change34/plc-cha34.pdf

Kruse, S., Seashore-Louis, K., & Bryk, A. (1994). Building professional community in schools. *Issues in Restructuring Schools, 6,* 3–6. http://dieppestaff.pbworks.com/w/file/fetch/66176267/Professional%20Learning%20communities.pdf

Kutash, J., Nico, E., Gorin, E., Rahmatullah, S., & Tallant, T. (2010). *The school turnaround field guide.* FSG Social Impact Advisors. http://www.wallacefoundation.org/knowledge-center/school-leadership/district-policy-and-practice/Documents/The-School-Turnaround-Field-Guide.pdf

Lane, K. L., Kalberg, J. R., & Menzies, H. M. (2009). *Developing schoolwide programs to prevent and manage problem behaviors: A step-by-step approach.* The Guilford Press.

Lezotte, L. W., & McKee Snyder, K. (2011). *What effective schools do: Re-envisioning the correlates.* Solution Tree.

Marzano, R. J., Heflebower, T., Hoegh, J. K., Warrick, P., & Grift, G. (2016). *Collaborative teams that transform schools: The next step in PLCs.* Marzano Research.

Marzano, R. J., Marzano, J. S., & Pickering, D. J. (2003). *Classroom management that works: Research based strategies for every teacher.* ASCD.

Marzano, R. J., Pickering, D. J., & Pollock, J. E. (2001). *Classroom instruction that works: Research based strategies for increasing student achievement* (1st ed.). ASCD.

National Policy Board for Educational Administration. (2015). *Professional standards for educational leaders 2015.* Author. https://ccsso.org/sites/default/files/2017-10/ProfessionalStandardsforEducationalLeaders2015forNPBEAFINAL.pdf or https://ccsso.org/resource-library/professional-standards-educational-leaders

Neuenswander, B. (2015). *Kansas state assessments: A footprint Fall 2015.* Kansas State Department of Education. http://www.kslegislature.org/li_2016/b2015_16/committees/ctte_spc_2015_special_committee_on_k12_student_s_1/documents/testimony/20151110_41.pdf

No Child Left Behind Act of 2001, 115 U.S.C. § 1425 (2002). https://www.congress.gov/107/plaws/publ110/PLAW-107publ110.htm

Pitler, H., Hubbell, E. R., & Kuhn, M. (2012). *Using technology with classroom instruction that works* (2nd ed.). McRel.

Senge, P. M. (2006). *The fifth discipline. The art and practice of the learning organization* (revised ed.). Doubleday.

Sergiovanni, T. J. (1992). *Moral leadership: Getting to the heart of school improvement.* Jossey-Bass.

Stronge, J. H. (2007). *Qualities of effective teachers* (2nd ed.). ASCD.

Watson, A. D. (2015). Design thinking for life. *Art Education, 68*(3), 12–16. https://doi.org/10.1080/00043125.2015.11519317

Whitaker, T. (2013). *What great teachers do differently: 17 things that matter most* (2nd ed.). Routledge.

Zepeda, S. (2011). *Professional development: What works* (2nd ed.). Eye on Education.

Zepeda, S. (2019). *Professional development: What works* (3rd ed.). Routledge.

Acknowledgments

This book acknowledges the educational leaders who stepped up to the plate school year after school year and took on the next, greatest new reform effort to move our schools from "Good to Great". You withstood change after change implementing standards-based learning, common core state standards, benchmark testing, cooperative learning trainings, differentiated instruction, and curricular additions including social/emotional learning, financial literacy, career and technical education exposing students to careers and real-world skills, increasing the schools' connectedness to the workplace. You became proficient at writing test items, co-creating criterion-referenced tests and standards-based report cards. You helped create our own bullying, technology acceptable use, crisis intervention, and drug-free school policies and plans. You accepted and realized change was inevitable. My role was to help bring clarity to the decision-making process with collaborative reason backing our actions.

Your willingness to participate and share what was working made the difference. You were willing to commit to the possibilities so our goals could be realized; we found success.

Many of you are entering another pivotal point in life called retirement, so it is with this book that I thank you for your dedication over the past 40 years, making a difference day by day, student by student! It's time we shared our gift, "how" we approached change and how our successes resulted in rapid sustainable change. We pay it forward to the next generation of educational leaders, the post-pandemic educators!

1

What is appreciative inquiry (AI)?

Appreciative inquiry (AI) is a results-based change model. The AI process helps people discover what's working and brings out the best in their organizations (Cooperrider et al., 2008). Educational change leaders will find this method or approach to change as a powerful decision-making tool that helps people discover what they appreciate and value about themselves, their school, or district.

The inquiry part of AI is an exploratory process where people imagine new possibilities through collaborative dialogue. The way questions are asked during the process is important because they are framed within a positive context that brings strength and inspiration to the group's potential or in the case of a school, the school's culture, as opposed to using deficit-based language.

The AI change process is a framework that helps people discover "who we are" and "what we want". The focus of the inquiry is centered on the potential or positive core, rather than approaching change through typical problem-solving models that focus on problems to be fixed. What the school or district values becomes the positive core or the central focus and is determined by the people involved in the process as they describe what they value and appreciate in each other and in their school; then, they imagine and express the possibilities of what the future could bring to the school or district. Facilitating change through AI involves both an understanding of the philosophy behind the AI results-based, change process and the actual step-by-step procedures, known as the 4-D cycle: Discovery, Dream, Design, and Destiny.

DOI: 10.4324/9781003350804-1

AI is a philosophy, or way of thinking

AI is a philosophy, or way of thinking with underlying principles that help educational leaders understand what it means to value, appreciate, and recognize the efforts and differences of others. The philosophy or underlying principles of AI emerge from the two root words used to name the change model: Appreciate and inquire. Appreciate means to value, to affirm, and to recognize the worth or significance; inquire means to explore, to seek information through questioning.

The philosophy or way of thinking is aligned to seeing the glass half full versus half empty, where the inquiry or questions are written using strengths-based language versus the more traditional problem-seeking questions asked with negative undertones. Establishing the underlying principles for AI will help in recognizing the differences between the AI approach and other change model efforts. Change efforts are a constant in education and understanding that a school is a learning organization brings perspective to the need for continual adaptation, refinement, transformation, and innovation.

AI reinforces the idea that schools are dynamic, learning organizations

The school is a learning organization (Senge, 2006) where the district's administrative team and teaching staff continuously work and learn together collectively to get the desired results; they are seen as a dynamic, ever-changing ecosystem. Students advance to the next grade level on a yearly basis. New students come from feeder schools. Teachers and administrators move in and out of the district, transfer, or retire with time. Demographics change. Buildings undergo grade level reconfigurations, are updated and remodeled, or closed. Yet, the stakeholders of the school's ecosystem or community—the educational leaders, parents, and students drive the learning process and possess the capacity to change the school and its culture. The central thought is that schools are learning organizations and the development of systems thinking begins with the interactions and communication of the people associated with the school and district.

The focus for the inquiry is on the learning unit like the district's administrative team. It could be a building leadership team, or a teacher team such as a professional learning community (PLC) within a school, a grade level team, the school's advisory council, the school improvement team, the entire school staff, or multiple school technology teams that comprise the district level technology committee. The AI learning unit could be the district's PreK-12 mathematics curriculum committee or the district's health and wellness team; the learning unit could be as large as several hundred people engaged in the district's strategic planning process or as small as two to three people working towards a common goal. This book focuses on helping the educational leaders at the school and district levels (typically the administrative team) learn how to facilitate and implement the rapid, change model known as AI with its 4-D cycle.

The power is held within the collective wisdom of the learning unit or team. People interacting with one another possess the capacity to grow, imagine, and change, which is what Senge (2006), an American systems' scientist, whose work has centered around shared leadership, meant by systems thinking or thinking systemically. The notion that organizational learning occurs in schools is based on the knowledge of the people, their capacity to grow and learn, and their perceptions of understanding. The skills used to facilitate the change process where AI is the decision-making model involves valuing and affirming the worth of others, dialoguing what should be, and innovating what could be. Change is a social learning process.

AI is a change process—a social learning process

AI is a change process that is highly participatory, relying on the involvement, communication, and social interactions from the people within the organization, or as is the focus for this book, the school setting. Bandura's (1971) social learning theory is based on the premise that people learn and imitate others based on observations. An elementary teacher spends a good deal of time observing students read, providing feedback, and in modeling, by reading out loud. The same is true for the adults in schools. They learn from each other by sharing lessons and resources; they have conversations with others, observe, adapt, and change based on their experiences and the experiences from others. Administrators and teachers talk about the changes they would like to see; they set goals and monitor progress. Conversations occur and relationships develop. Meaning is constructed from relationships, from interconnectedness, which becomes reality. The words educational leaders use, and ideas they believe create their world.

Through the AI process, reality is socially created through collaboration, based on the shared conversations, stories, dreams, and aspirations they have for their students, their teacher team, their school, or district. Once the questioning or inquiry process is initiated, ideas and possibilities are generated. The vision or path becomes clear, people accept responsibility for the decisions, and commit to the action required; the change process is set in motion. Change in a learning organization is a social learning process, and the power to transform comes from within the learning unit of the organization— the people connected and involved in the change process.

AI empowers people to achieve excellence from within the organization

The power to achieve excellence comes from within the organization. The organizational life of each school, district, building leadership team, PLC, or teacher team is a story that can be told. The power to achieving excellence is found from within the learning unit—whether it be your teacher team, your school's staff, or your district's administrative team.

Think about your school's story. What is the history of the school? What is the school known for and why? How was the school given its name? Tell a story about your involvement in the district, school, or teacher team. Based on the various roles within a school organization (e.g., superintendent, building principal, general education teacher, counselor, lunchroom supervisor, custodian) each person has a different story.

The building principal tells her story about making a difference by supporting the learning ideas for improving reading fluency with the third-grade teachers. A fifth-grade teacher brings a story to share with his peer coaching triad/team about vocabulary development with data that shows student growth in reading. The memorable, past stories help bring light to best practices and what works. Appreciating and valuing the stories and conversations lead to imagining what is possible for a more desirable future.

The power to create your own roadmap or step-by-step playbook to excellence is within you, your administrative teams, building leadership teams, teacher teams, school staff, or district level committees. The AI process is the vehicle or method for sharing stories of best practices of what works and how excellence is being achieved, creating the idealized images for future learning. Like the Kansas sunflower that moves with the sunlight, the direction you and your colleagues choose creates your destiny, the preferred future.

Success is based in having a change strategy or model that works. For the purposes of this book, the approach or change model is known as the AI method. The AI method has a 4-D cycle, which involves a step-by-step process that provides a focused direction for the district's administrative team, the school's building leadership team, or a teacher team that sets participants up for success and achieving excellence, since collectively, the decisions made, control your destiny—the co-constructed, preferred future.

AI empowers people from within the organization to achieve excellence. Ultimately, the story you tell about the organization (district, school, teacher team) projects a visual to others. The likelihood of the organization's success is based on the choices you and your team make. The first step is a willingness to participate in the change process. Excitement builds as those involved in the process connect with each other, share the best of what works, and envision what might be, as they move toward shared goals and operationalize the vision for the desired future. One of the outcomes of the AI process is that it promotes the synergy of others.

AI promotes the synergy of others

Jon Gordon, author of *The Energy Bus* (2007) used the shark among swimmers analogy to help visualize the challenges, situations, and problems a person deals with whether at work or homelife. Every person has battles and roadblocks, but how one reacts to those events is what makes the difference. Choosing to be positive is an intentional outcome. Maybe you can relate to having attended a meeting full of complaints where you felt totally drained from the negativity and nothing seemed to have been accomplished. People prefer to avoid such meetings. Opposite to that is a meeting full of positive energy that has focus where you are engaged, exchanging ideas, and expressing possibilities. The AI method or process recognizes that every person has strengths and contributes in some way.

People are the biggest asset to an organization (Abdollahzadeh, 2013). There is something that works in every school—there is good in every school, every person. Each person has a choice in how they act and react, making a difference by being positive or negative. Attitudes are the way we respond to others and to situations. Attitudes can be framed within a positive mindset. Attitudes can be reframed by looking at an issue from various perspectives or views. The power of being positive is a way of being (seeing the glass half full, rather than half empty) and is an important part of the philosophy or underlying principle of AI (Cooperrider et al., 2003). A positive mindset will help spread the level of energy among those in your district; you will find that changing your mindset from mere coping day to day to practicing the principles of AI will help you find personal growth as you envision the future possibilities for your teachers, as you establish a positive school environment, or enhance the communication levels of the district leadership team.

The AI process helps you use your energies in a constructive way and recognize your talents and abilities to achieve the change you want to see in yourself, your school, or district. AI asks the question, "What do we look like when we are performing our best?" The inquiry focuses on our potential, generating what our best looks like. The AI change process requires dialogue, sharing what is possible. Creating a shared vision promotes a powerful synergy—a momentum of hope, inspiration, and empowerment that results in action. The action becomes the change. The change model itself is an iterative process that goes through four steps, which can be repeated over and over as the topic of inquiry or questions change.

AI is a change model with four steps: discovery, dream, design, and destiny

AI is a change model with four distinct steps known as the 4-D cycle: Discovery, Dream, Design, and Destiny. The "4-D" cycle was introduced to business leaders in the 1980s by David Cooperrider as an alternative to the traditional problem-solving approach for organizational change and has become one of the most popular initiatives to transform current organizational conditions (Cooperrider et al., 2003). Figure 1.1 illustrates the 4-D cycle used in the AI change model. There are four steps in the 4-D cycle:

Discovery: Describe the best from the past or the best from "what is", what works, what we value.
Dream: Imagine new possibilities for a preferred future.
Design: Transform the preferred future into action.
Destiny: Action planning and commitments to the plans of what will be.

Figure 1.1 shows the AI "4-D" cycle: Discovery, Dream, Design, and Destiny phases.

The AI change model is really a two-pronged approach, the philosophy, or way of thinking with a positive mindset, and then the four steps, known as the 4-D cycle. To see change in your organization, whether that be at the district, the school, or a smaller unit such as the grade level team, high school math department, or a PLC, the AI approach is like a learning and training program. The more you learn about the AI philosophy, or way of thinking, and the more you participate in the four steps in the 4-D cycle, the easier the desired results become for your team, school, or district.

The AI process really is a cultural transformation when people begin to change their wiring from a negative mindset with problems to be solved to a more collaborative effort, being open to imagining possibilities as to what

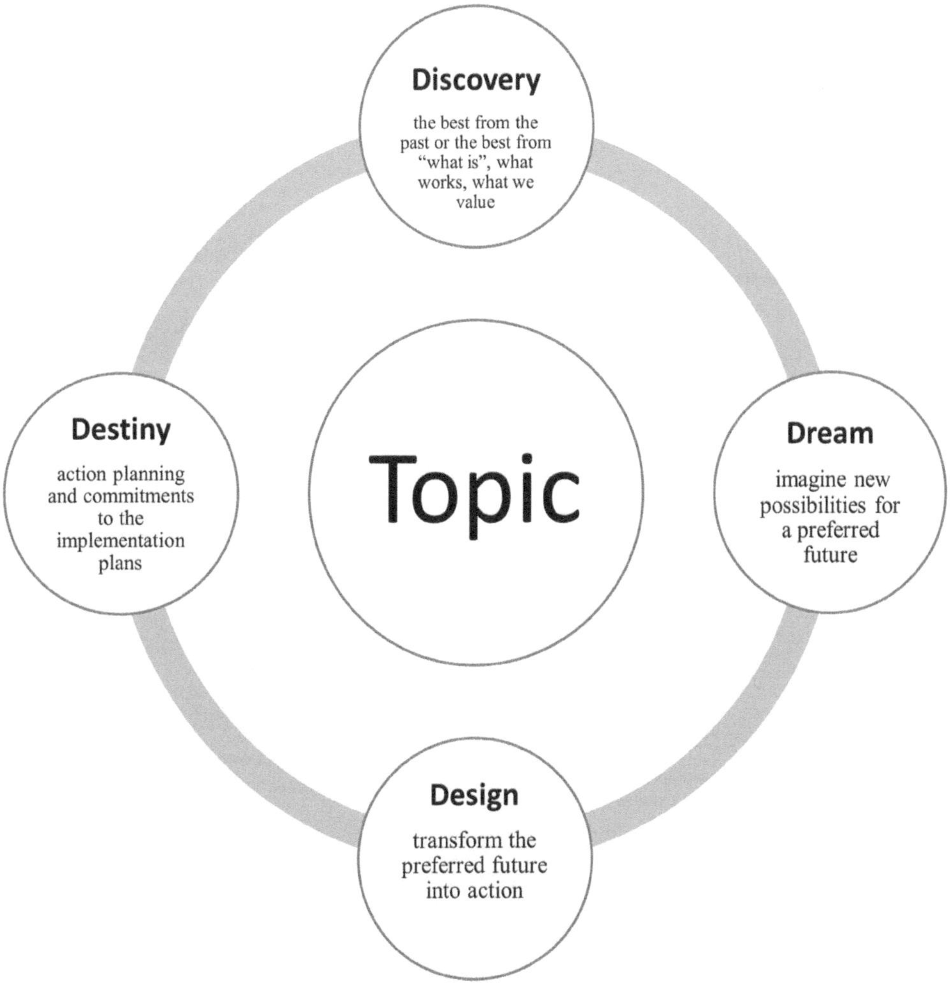

Figure 1.1 The AI 4-D cycle change model.

could be, then working toward a preferred future with common purpose and goals. The result of the AI change process is co-constructing a clear vision, then establishing achievable goals. You are the key to your success and the success of your district's administrative team, building leadership team, or teacher team.

References

Abdollahzadeh, M. (2013). Empowerment and organizational change. *International Research Journal of Applied and Basic Sciences*, 4(1), 1–5. https://irjabs.com/files_site/paperlist/r_603_130116131933.pdf

Bandura, A. (1971). *Social learning theory*. General Learning Press. http://www.esludwig.com/uploads/2/6/1/0/26105457/bandura_sociallearningtheory.pdf

Cooperrider, D. L., Whitney, D., & Stavros, J. M. (2003). *Appreciative inquiry handbook: The first in a series of AI workbooks for leaders of change* (1st ed.). Lakeshore.

Cooperrider, D. L., Whitney, D., Stavros, J. M., & Fry, R. (2008). *The appreciative inquiry Handbook: For leaders of change*. Crown Custom.

Gordon, J. (2007). *The energy bus: 10 rules to fuel your life, work, and team with positive energy*. John Wiley & Sons.

Senge, P. M. (2006). *The fifth discipline. The art and practice of the learning organization*. Doubleday.

2

Why choose AI as the change model for decision-making?

The appreciative inquiry (AI) 4-D change model is used for many reasons, but mainly because the process works. It is known worldwide and is used in a variety of organizations. The decision-making process involves everyone, is solutions-based, brings clarity to the next steps, expedites change, and is a much more peaceful solution than the traditional problem-solving models. The AI change model is proactive, focused on a positive mindset using strengths-based language, where shared decision-making and the degree of participation becomes a matter of personal choice and responsibility. The AI change process with the four-step, 4-D cycle offers a guiding framework where people work collaboratively to solve their problems and issues. It then becomes a matter of personal responsibility whether to act and commit to a preferred future.

Reasons to use the AI process include it being a change model with simple, defined four-steps where the number of people involved in the shared decision-making process can be two people or 200 or more than 2,000. The AI change model has the capacity to hear all voices regardless of rank or position in the organization, so it is non-hierarchical. The process does involve communicating with one another where learning occurs by listening and sharing—it is a collaborative effort. Once those involved understand the thinking behind AI and the AI 4-D steps, the rate of change becomes expedited. Several reasons for using the AI change model with the four-step process are detailed in this chapter. The first reason to select the AI change model is because it is a solutions-focused process that uses strengths-based language.

DOI: 10.4324/9781003350804-2

Why? Because AI is a solutions-focused process, using strengths-based language

The language used throughout the AI change model follows "seeing the cup half full" mindset, so the questions asked are written in a positive sense, thus the term strengths-based, rather than deficit-based language. When something goes wrong or does not work out well, many times the default is to go to a negative option, placing blame on external factors and pointing fingers at others. Words exchanged may be harsh and cause division; people tend to become defensive and retreat or avoid each other, which in turn, fragments and destroys the trust among the team. Few people step up and try to fix the problem, and in doing so, it typically becomes a band aid approach to smooth over the failure. Regardless of the fault or misunderstanding, the deficit-based choice of words is draining and leaves people with a gloomy view. Kegan and Laskow-Lahey (2001) encourage people to move from the language of blame to the language of personal responsibility.

The words we use matter and are a personal choice. Words spoken become those a person owns; they are responsible for what is said. The AI change model provides opportunity for personal responsibility with a plethora of choices:

> choice in attitude.
> choice to participate and to what extent.
> choice to share stories.
> choice to be actively committed to future possibilities.

The extent of a person's involvement in the AI process is a matter of personal choice and responsibility. Becoming proactive and more optimistic through a positive mindset helps pave the way to excellence, drawing out the best in you and your team.

Tschannen-Moran and Tschannen-Moran (2011) found, "by getting people to focus on their strengths, AI changes the conversations from complaining to celebrating" (p. 444). Rather than dreading the next faculty meeting, think in a positive mindset using strengths-based words about the most successful staff or administrative meeting you have ever attended. The AI positive or strengths-based mindset asks, what made the meeting successful? Who was involved? What steps could be taken to have more staff or administrative meetings like that? You can be a part of the solution as you develop a sense of personal responsibility, making a difference based on your choices and actions. The AI choice for a change method provides the framework but laying the foundation to building a better future begins with the words we choose when communicating with others.

Why? Because AI provides the framework for solving our own issues

The assumption is that as educational leaders, we can solve our own issues, and we are capable of learning new skills. Wheatley (2002) believes "people are the solution to the problems that confront us…relationships are all there is" (p. 19). She says, "the future comes from where we are now. It materializes from the actions, values, and beliefs we're practicing now. We're creating the future each day, by what we choose to do" (Wheatley, 2002, p. 64).

Change is a constant, and adapting is inevitable. By taking personal responsibility for our actions, choices, and decisions in the present, we can create the future we want. Change is a process and using a change model where participation is encouraged, where ideas can be expressed regardless of position, and where collective decision-making is valued is the center of the AI change model. The AI process provides the framework for change through opportunity and participation from those within the system, creating the conditions and allowances for commitment to discover solutions within the team, school, or district. The change model is based on a simple four-step process known as the 4-D cycle which is results-based, creating a desired future from those within the system who participate.

Why? Because AI is a simple four-step cycle focused on continuous improvement

The AI process encourages a proactive way of thinking, and it comes with a simple four-step process known as the 4-D cycle: Discovery, Dream, Design, and Destiny. Becoming familiar with the four steps will help guide discussions that lead to possibilities and collaborative solutions. The power to change comes from within the school's organization—the individuals, their abilities to communicate and work together toward common goals. Identifying and having a change model that team members are familiar with helps everyone involved know what is happening and have a voice as to why the change is needed and what change needs to happen. It brings clarity to the change process. The goal in the AI change model is to transition from the idealized future to making it the present. The 4-D cycle is iterative; the practice of using the 4-D cycle can be repeated so continual improvement, progress, and monitoring can be achieved.

Why? Because AI participants can range from one to two people to 100s of people

The number of participants involved in the AI process can range from one or two individuals to hundreds of people as they work through the decision-making process toward common, prioritized goals and solutions. A single person can engage in the process for self-improvement setting their own goals such as in the case of a building principal or teacher reflecting on his/her own evaluation process. The AI change model works well when school personnel work in smaller groups such as an elementary grade level teacher team of three or four people. The AI 4-D cycle works well with high school departments with 15–16 teachers; it works well with a school staff of 40–50 people within one building or when developing leadership capacity among the district's leadership team.

The process in the AI change model works when multiple schools need to collaborate for decision-making initiatives like the adoption of district-wide or K-12 curriculum or determining how to deliver curriculum in a blended/hybrid online setting or in a totally remote setting. The process has proven successful when the community is invited to participate in district-wide strategic planning events with 150–200 people. The AI model includes all stakeholders in the process, thus becoming a non-hierarchical, collaborative decision-making, change effort.

Why? Because the AI change model is a non-hierarchical, collaborative effort

The AI model includes everyone who wants or needs to be involved in the decision-making process. It flattens the idea of a hierarchy where everyone is seen as an equal, being on the same level regardless of their role in the school or district. The process is highly participatory where sharing past experiences and stories helps bring about the good in what has worked and what is valued by the participants. Intentionally focusing on the good helps create a positive mental state about you and your work with others.

Knowing what has worked and what is working helps bring perspective to the current situation, issue, or problem of practice. The emphasis is on collaboration and working toward solutions with renewed images of what could be possible for the future of the district, the administrative leadership for each school, the fourth-grade teacher team, or the high school math department. The AI change model with its highly, participatory process helps administrative teams and staff develop bonds, bringing together diverse voices, a shared sense of becoming a community of learners through shared stories and experiences with an openness to new ideas and visions of future possibilities with the result being a co-constructed image that becomes a reality.

Why? Because the AI 4-D cycle is a results-oriented, rapid decision-making process that expedites change

Knowledge of the AI process helps expedite change. The learners who participate and experience the AI process work with a common purpose of moving toward a shared ideology and commitment to the changes or solutions as they realize what is possible for the district, school, grade level team, or department. The result is that they co-create the change; they co-construct a desired future. When participants become familiar with the AI 4-D cycle, there is clarity in the change process. The guess work is omitted, and people are held accountable for their decisions because the participants create and own their story. The AI change method is results-oriented.

As participants work through the AI 4-D cycle, they become a purposeful community; they work collaboratively through the decision-making process with purpose and focus as common goals are formed, creating the changes necessary to make the desired future a reality. Sergiovanni (1994) says purposeful communities are "places where members have developed a community of mind that bonds them together in special ways and binds them to a shared ideology" (p. 72). The AI process involves the co-construction of common goals and helps bring about the change needed to realize the shared vision or goals.

The AI process is relationship-based where those participating in the process form a common bond, which helps accelerate the change process when what is valued becomes known and participants are united, committed, and dedicated to the co-constructed plan. They learn that the AI process involves sharing past stories and experiences, bridging the past to the future by imagining possibilities and planning next steps. When administrators and staff become familiar with the AI 4-D cycle as the preferred method for change, they can work with staff in a quick manner and respond to a rapidly changing environment in a positive and resilient manner, leading to a dynamic learning organization.

Why? Because the AI process leads to the formation of a true learning organization

The AI process leads to the formation of the school as a true learning organization. Senge (2006) defined learning organizations as those where members continuously work and learn together collectively to get the desired results. The AI process serves as the vehicle where learning and development occur. Those involved learn by sharing stories, breaking down barriers with the exchange of ideas and flow of information; they learn about the organization (the school, their teacher team or administrative team, the district), learn what is valued, and envision a future of what could be, and commit to common goals. It leads to staff buy-in, commitment, and dedication.

The focus of the AI process is on leadership development, both administrators and teachers, who are committed to learning from each other; therefore, it is a shared leadership framework. A true learning organization exhibits the qualities of having a collaborative learning culture where individuals are valued and have a role in the bigger picture of the organization, work collectively developing a shared vision with a free exchange of knowledge and ideas, and have a continual learning mindset (Senge, 2006).

District administrative and building leadership teams lean toward what works—best practices, evidence-based or research-based practices. The practice of using a solutions-based option as a change method like AI has proven to be a more effective intervention, rather than the alternative problems-based option (Peelle III, 2006). Organizations that use AI practices show more resilience and optimism. Veryleysen et al.'s (2015) study encourages organizations to use the AI process because "engaging in AI practices greatly fulfills people's three basic psychological needs for competence, autonomy, and relatedness" (p. 30). They found that participation in the AI process helps develop and has shown increases in one's confidence, hope, optimism, and resilience calling it enhancing a person's "psychological capital" (Veryleysen et al., 2015, p. 30).

The AI process, which is results-oriented, focused on creating a culture of change, also becomes a breeding ground for professional success where personal excellence, hope, optimism, and innovation are valued as the school or district moves toward becoming a true learning organization. Many types of businesses and organizations including school districts and universities have been using AI and the 4-D cycle worldwide.

Why? Because AI is a proven, change model used worldwide

Businesses, municipalities, governmental agencies, nonprofits, school districts, and universities around the world reported past experiences with problem-solving models with little to no success in sustaining change or making improvements within their organizations but have found the AI approach to be a much more viable option due to the collaborative efforts and possibilities shared for future endeavors (COMPASS, 2003; Hung et al., 2018). The AI approach helps develop a positive mindset that is more favorable for establishing motivation, which provides the basis for employees to work together for the greater good of the organization (Spindler & Van den brul, 2003).

The founder of the AI change model and decision-making process, David Cooperrider, began his research in 1986 with a medical clinic group of doctors in Cleveland, OH (Cooperrider et al., 2008). Since then, the medical field has used the AI approach extensively especially in bridging the gap between practice and theory and in discovering ways to provide and sustain high quality care (Hung et al., 2018; Magnussen et al., 2019).

Businesses such as Roadway Express in Akron, OH (Ludema & Fry, 2008), British Broadcasting Corporation (Spindler & Van den brul, 2003) McDonalds, and John Deere (Ludema et al., 2003; Whitney & Trosten-Bloom, 2003) have used AI to improve operations. Cities such as Chicago, IL (Browne, 1998, 2009), Dubuque, IA (Finegold et al., 2002) and City of Hampton, VA (Johnson & Leavitt, 2001) have used AI as a proactive, participatory process to establish a collective effort for city planning and future directionality.

Governmental agencies like state correctional facilities (Frerich & Murphy-Nugen, 2019) and the Department of Children and Families (Walton, 2018) have relied on AI to help improve processes with interrelated agencies in meeting the needs of constituents. The US Navy used the AI 4-D cycle to help improve leadership and expedite change (Tripp & Zipsie, 2002).

Religious organizations include the Catholic church (Blanchard, 2017) where the AI process was used to promote volunteerism, and the Church of Pentecost (Quainoo, 2020) used AI to identify strengths and integrate community outreach programs. Various nonprofits such as the United Way and the Red Cross (Drabczyk, 2009; Whitney & Trosten-Bloom, 2003) have used AI for strategic planning purposes and in determining the values of those working and volunteering within the organization. Catholic Relief Services used

AI among African nations to facilitate peace, resolve land disputes, moving toward social cohesion in their efforts to sustain communities (Broemmelsiek, 2017).

School districts and universities have used AI to help advance team building efforts, leadership development, strategic planning, and address systemic issues intentionally that improve practice and change policy. San Martin and Calabrese (2012) used AI as a strengths-based approach to help improve the perceptions of an alternative high school. Brooks (2016) used AI as the preferred approach to determine social skills needed to maintain employment among students with learning disabilities; Rowley (2017) discovered qualities of high performing elementary teacher teams by using the AI 4-D cycle. Zant (2019) used AI's discovery and dream steps in the change model to help raise awareness levels among transitioning, dually graduating high school students from respective community colleges to entrance into four-year higher education institutions where entrance meant "junior year, not freshmen year".

Presidents/CEOs, executives, and educational leaders from organizations around the world have praised the AI approach and many have shared quotes and experiences, detailing what the change model has meant to them, to the culture of their organization, and their businesses. Whether it be testimony from the United Nations' secretary general, the global vice president of Whole Foods Market, or a professor at Columbia University, the AI process with its 4-D cycle has provided an alternative approach to problem-solving that is solutions-based around the world (Praise for AI, n.d.).

The next question to address then, is how can I use the AI approach with the 4-D cycle to make a difference with those I work with…to make a difference with the school staff…to make a difference with leadership development among the district's administrative team? Chapter 3 provides the roadmap or playbook, with step-by-step or play-by-play solutions.

References

Blanchard, K. (2017). *Improving the ministry of pastoral care during a transitional change in leadership at a Catholic church.* (Publication No. 10742975) [Doctoral dissertation, Saint Mary's College, CA] Proquest Dissertations and Theses Global. https://www.proquest.com/openview/5059ee30486c3ee d8354d9505b3b10e6/1?pq-origsite=gscholar&cbl=18750&diss=y

Broemmelsiek, M. (2017). *The ties that bind: Building social cohesion in divided communities.* Catholic Relief Services. https://www.crs.org/sites/default/files/toolsresearch/crs_ties_rev-08-03-2017_web.pdf

Brooks, J. L. (2016). *An appreciative inquiry into the social skills an individual with disabilities uses to maintain employment*. (Publication No. 10599241) [Doctoral dissertation, Southwestern College-Kansas]. ProQuest Dissertations. https://media.proquest.com/media/hms/ORIG/2/Mz3fI?_s=svIw%2FmTiCTWUVKSAoqwMIXt UvIM%3D

Browne, B. W. (1998). Imagine Chicago. In S. A. Hammond, & C. Royal (Eds.), *Lessons from the field* (pp. 76–89). Practical Press.

Browne, B. W. (2009). Part 2: Intergenerational conversations in communities. An inspired future: The significance of city-wide conversations in Chicago. *AI Practitioner, 11*(2), 28–33. https://www.imaginechicago.org/-videos-case-studies-publications-discussions

Community Partnerships for Sustainable Resource Management in Malawi (COMPASS). (2003). *Introduction to appreciative inquiry: Training Manual Workshop for NGOs and Government Departments Held in Blantyre, Malawi: March 31 – April 8, 2003*. COMPASS. https://pdf.usaid.gov/pdf_docs/PNADB195.pdf

Cooperrider, D. L., Whitney, D., Stavros, J. M., & Fry, R. (2008). *The appreciative inquiry Handbook: For leaders of change*. Crown Custom.

Drabczyk, A. (2009). American Red Cross Academy: Team-building and leadership development. *Journal of Social Change, 3*, 1–14. https://scholarworks.waldenu.edu/cgi/viewcontent.cgi?article=1002&context=jsc

Finegold, M. A., Holland, B. M., & Lingham, T. (2002). Appreciative inquiry and public dialogue: An approach to community change. *Public Organization Review, 2*(3), 235–252. https://doi.org/10.1023/A:1020292413486

Frerich, M. A., & Murphy-Nugen, A. B. (2019). Women's voices: An appreciative inquiry of off-site postsecondary correctional education. *Journal of Women and Social Work, 34*(1) 8–27. https://doi.org/10.1177/0886109918796250

Hung, L., Phinney, A., Chaudhury, H., Rodney, P., Tabamo, J., & Bohl, D. (2018). Appreciative inquiry: Bridging research and practice in a hospital setting. *International Journal of Qualitative Methods, 17*, 1–10. https://doi.org/10.1177/1609406918769444

Johnson, G., & Leavitt, W. (2001). Building on success: Transforming organizations through an appreciative inquiry. *Public Personnel Management, 30*(1), 129–136. https://link.gale.com/apps/doc/A73555065/AONE?u=klnb_fhsuniv&sid=bookmarkAONE&xid=4b7a8653

Kegan, R., & Laskow-Lahey, L. (2001). *How the way we talk can change the way we work*. Jossey-Bass.

Ludema, J. D., & Fry, R. E. (2008). The practice of appreciative inquiry. In P. Reason, & H. Bradbury (Eds.), *The SAGE handbook of action research* (pp. 280–296). SAGE. https://dx.doi.org/10.4135/9781848607934.n27

Ludema, J. D., Whitney, D., Mohr, B. J., & Griffin, T. J. (2003). *The appreciative inquiry summit: A practitioner's guide for leading large-group change.* Berrett-Koehler.

Magnussen, I-L., Alteren, J., & Bondas, T. (2019). Appreciative inquiry in a Norwegian nursing home: A unifying and maturing process to forward new knowledge and new practice. *International Journal of Qualitative Studies on Health and Well-Being, 14*(1), 1–12. https://doi.org/10.1080/17482631.2018.1559437

Peelle III, H. E. (2006). Appreciative inquiry and creative problem solving in cross-functional teams. *The Journal of Applied Behavioral Science, 42*(4), 447–467. https://doi-org.ezproxy.fhsu.edu/10.1177/0021886306292479

Praise for AI. (n.d.). Case Western Reserve University, Weatherhead School of Management. *Praise for Appreciative Inquiry.* https://weatherhead.case.edu/core-topics/appreciative-inquiry/praise

Quainoo, J. M. (2020). *Implementing the appreciative inquiry approach to revitalize the Church of Pentecost Canada.* Tyndale University. https://digitalcollections.tyndale.ca/bitstream/handle/20.500.12730/178/Quainoo_James_McKeown_D_Min_2020.pdf?sequence=4&isAllowed=y

Rowley, L. (2017). *An appreciative inquiry: Valuing elementary teacher team relationships as the balance to the educational ecosystem* [Unpublished doctoral dissertation]. Southwestern College-Kansas.

San Martin, T. L. & Calabrese, R. L. (2012). Empowering at-risk students through appreciative inquiry. *The International Journal of Educational Management, 25*(2), 110–123. https://doi.org/10.1108/09513541111107542

Senge, P. M. (2006). *The fifth discipline. The art and practice of the learning organization.* (revised ed.). Doubleday.

Sergiovanni, T. J. (1994). *Building community in schools.* Jossey-Bass.

Spindler, S., & Van den brul, C. (2003). *Making it happen, creativity, and audiences: A BBC case study.* NHK Broadcasting Studies. https://www.nhk.or.jp/bunken/english/reports/pdf/06-07_no5_03.pdf

Tripp, P., & Zipsie, M. (2002). *The introduction of appreciative inquiry to the U.S. Navy using appreciative inquiry interviews and the large group intervention with applications to U.S. Marine Corps logistics strategic management.* (Publication No.109456006) [Doctoral dissertation, Naval Postgraduate School-Monterey, CA]. Calhoun, The NPS Institutional Archive. https://calhoun.nps.edu/handle/10945/6006

Tschannen-Moran, M., & Tschannen-Moran, B. (2011). Taking a strengths-based focus improves school climate. *Journal of School Leadership, 21*(3), 422–448. https://link.gale.com/apps/doc/A259381185/AONE?u=klnb_fhsuniv&sid=bookmark-AONE&xid=5d4fe63f

Veryleysen, B., Lambrechts, F., & Van Acker, F. (2015). Building psychological capital with appreciative inquiry: Investigating the mediating role of basic psychological need satisfaction. *The Journal of Applied Behavioral Science*, 51(1), 10–35. https://doi.org/10.1177/0021886314540209

Walton, G. (2018). *An appreciative inquiry evaluation of the statewide racial justice workgroup's efforts*. (Publication No. 10784145 b) [Doctoral dissertation, Cappella University]. ProQuest Dissertations.

Wheatley, M. J. (2002). *Turning to one another: Simple conversations to restore hope to the future*. Berrett-Koehler.

Whitney, D., & Trosten-Bloom, A. (2003). *The power of appreciative inquiry: A practical guide to positive change*. Berrett-Koehler.

Zant, K. (2019). *An appreciative inquiry into dually graduating students' transition to four-year institutions*. (Publication No. 13886814) [Doctoral dissertation, Southwestern College-Kansas]. ProQuest Dissertations Publishing. https://search.proquest.com/openview/6d5d22d9ab007a09fe2ee1372aa98ef5/1?pq-origsite=gscholar&cbl=51922&diss=y

3

How to facilitate change using the AI 4-D cycle

How does a school district superintendent or a building principal implement change or respond to mandates that require change? Educational leaders are often confronted with issues such as,

> how to provide a safe school environment.
> how to address systems that propagate inequities.
> how to create a diverse and inclusive culture.
> how to address the staffing crisis.
> how to coach leadership development with your administrative team, or
> how to implement a school-wide or even a district-wide prevention
> framework such as positive behavioral interventions and supports
> (PBIS).

There are emergency situations a school or district must confront in a timely manner, as well. How does a district switch from face-to-face learning to remote or online learning or offer blended learning during a pandemic? How does a district or school deal with a natural disaster and the aftermath? The school or district administrator is frequently looked at as having the answers. The answer lies with the educational leader having a proactive *go-to* change process.

Educational leaders need a change process to address the problems or issues that arise. They need a change model or framework that works, one that becomes repetitively practiced, guiding the decision-making process so

DOI: 10.4324/9781003350804-3

changes and initiatives can be addressed—one that has a step-by-step "how to" process to make the necessary changes. To make changes, the educational leader needs a game plan, so this chapter guides you through the appreciative inquiry (AI) process explaining step-by-step the purposes, goals, and tasks in the AI 4-D cycle: Discovery, Dream, Design, and Destiny. The AI 4-D cycle is a tool that provides the framework for change, the game plan. The examples take form like a coach's playbook.

The playbook

Winning coaches often use a playbook (Polk, 1982; Self, 2020). A playbook is frequently associated with coaching where you have a game plan. The game plan takes time to put together after reviewing and reflecting on the past game's performance including analysis of individual and team statistics. After the game, the coaches prepare for the next game reviewing videos and conducting a performance assessment of the next opponent.

Coaches revise the playbook after each game forming a different game plan that includes new plays that are learned during practices; the coaches script practices and continue to reinforce the routine plays (e.g., in basketball, a free throw does not change; in baseball, the player learns to move back on a fly ball, knowing it is easier to run forward than backward, or to help players anticipate the ball being hit to you, learning to stay low since it is easier to get up rather than back down), and establish a new set of goals for individuals, while simultaneously playing on the strengths of the team members. The coaches communicate the goals and hold the players and team accountable.

After the game, the process repeats itself where the game plan is revised, and new plays and goals are established to improve both individual and team performance. Each person has a role in the team, the individual's role is combined with other roles to fulfill the requirements needed to make the play; multiple plays during the game are likened to the steps being taken or the plan's process; then, the process or overall game plan becomes the playbook.

The playbook is the endgame or result after having completed the AI 4-D cycle. When applied to the AI approach, roles are defined such as the superintendent, the building principals, the classroom teacher, the librarian, or the counselor in the school. The roles are the individuals who need to be involved in the decision-making, change process based on the topic of inquiry. The topic of inquiry is the focus for using the AI 4-D change process. Participants in the AI 4-D discovery phase share their most memorable stories and experiences with the organization—whether at the school or district level. The plays are defined when there is an opportunity to share what works and envision a future together where improvements are possibilities and become the dream phase in the AI process.

The power is in the game plan dynamics which combines the work, vision, objectives, and outcomes of everyone involved in the process. The game plan is the design phase, determining what is going to happen. The product, or overall action plan, is the playbook that brings the collaborative efforts together and is known as the destiny. The solution or the "how" is found in AI—a systemic, proactive change model that is team based and highly participatory. Before participating in the AI process, the focus or topic for inquiry must be determined.

The topic or focus of inquiry

The first step is determining the topic of inquiry for change. The topic determines what the team will focus on, learn about, and improve upon to reach success. Figure 3.1 shows the topic as central to the purpose for engaging in an AI solutions-based change process; the topic sets the stage or provides the direction to be taken with the 4-D cycle.

When considering the topic of inquiry, ask, what are you trying to accomplish in your district with your administrative teams, building leadership teams, or teacher teams? If increasing teacher retention (reducing teacher turnover) were the topic or focus, then the 4-D cycle begins with the discovery phase, where those participating in the process would share the best from the past or what is currently working, such as best practices that keep teachers in the district or what they value about being a part of the district. The AI process focuses on strengths and assets, rather than on deficits. Fine (2022) argues that "those who are spearheading educational change should start by focusing on assets rather than deficits" (p. 3).

Figure 3.1 shows the topic or focus of inquiry in the center circle with the 4Ds in an outer circle. Once the topic has been established, the first phase, known as the discovery phase, begins the AI 4-D cycle process.

The topic is the focus for change, innovation, or renewal. It is important to frame the topic in the affirmative such as teacher retention, rather than teacher dropout or turnover. The topic may be worded as a deficit issue but needs to be restated in an affirmative manner. Table 3.1 provides examples where the topic is written in both deficit-based and strength-based language. Once the topic of inquiry for change has been determined, the next decision is to determine who needs to be involved in the AI 4-D cycle.

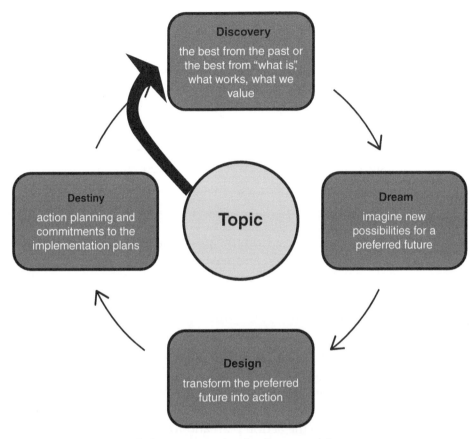

Figure 3.1 The AI 4-D cycle with the topic central to the change model process.

Table 3.1 Examples of topic selection written in the affirmative

Deficit-Based Topic	Strength-Based Topic
Teacher turnover	Teacher retention and attracting high quality staff
Failing school	High performing school
High dropout rates	100% graduation rate
Staff training needs	Meaningful staff development

Table 3.1 provides example topics using deficit-based and strength-based language. The topic chosen is reframed and written in an affirmative or positive manner and identifies the focus for the AI.

Four steps in the AI 4-D cycle

Once the topic of inquiry or area of focus has been determined and the participants have been identified as being contributors to the topic, then the discovery phase of the AI 4-D process begins as noted in Figure 3.1. The four D's in the AI 4-D cycle refer to Discovery, Dream, Design, and Destiny. The following four steps, along with descriptions are used when learning how to proceed with the AI process:

1 Discovery:
   a. Share stories (the best from the past) related to the topic to discover strengths, values, and wishes.
   b. Identify themes (what made those past experiences outstanding) and begin to map the positive core by sharing what's most valued or the core beliefs, best practices, strengths.
2 Dream:
   a. Imagine future possibilities of what could be.
   b. Prioritize and gain consensus of what should be.
3 Design: Create bold vision statements (provocative propositions) of an idealized future.
4 Destiny: Commit to the action plan and to sustaining the plan, making it happen!

Step 1: Discovery

Discovery phase: the magic in storytelling

The discovery phase includes two parts. The first part provides an opportunity for the participants to share stories (the best from the past) related to the topic to discover strengths, values, and wishes. The second part of the discovery phase is to identify themes (what made those past experiences outstanding) so the team can begin to map the positive core by sharing what's most valued or the core beliefs, best practices, and strengths.

Sharing stories

Each person involved in the AI process has unique perspectives and experiences based on their association with the school or district. A district administrator or building principal, facilitating the AI 4-D change model process may have teachers share stories and experiences that help the group understand more fully what attracts teachers to the district or community. One teacher may be a third generation born and raised in the community with many stories to share where he, his parents, and grandparents attended school; that teacher continues to have new experiences with a different lens as a parent with children enrolled in one or more of the schools. Another participant may be a first-year teacher, recently married, whose husband is a nurse at the local hospital. The couple are new to the community and have had very little experience with the schools or community. Both have valuable stories to share. They have past experiences and outstanding moments to share, and both teachers can share what they like, value, and envision for an ideal future. Sharing positives about the district may come from a building principal who has worked in multiple school districts who shares what sets this school system apart from the others. The educational leaders facilitating the change process may choose participants based on who they feel will be positive contributors to the topic of inquiry or focus for change.

The AI 4-D cycle discovery phase asks that the participants share their best stories from the past, the best from what is, what works, and express what they value, and wish for the future. Typically, there are four types of questions asked during the AI 4-D cycle discovery phase:

a past, personal story,
an outstanding moment or high point experience within the organization,
what is valued, and
three wishes.

Table 3.2 provides two example sets on different topics that depict the four types of guiding questions used in the AI 4-D discovery phase. The two example topics are developing a more focused and productive middle school math team/PLC and developing a more cohesive Board of Education. Table 3.3 provides two more example sets with the topics focused on creating a three-year, district strategic plan and establishing school level and district level technology vision and plans.

In Example Set 1, Table 3.2, the building administrator asks questions focused on discovering how to guide the 6th-7th-8th grade middle school

Table 3.2 The four types of questions asked during the AI 4-D cycle discovery phase with Example Sets 1 and 2

Discovery (Roles)	Discovery Questions Example Set 1	Discovery Questions Example Set 2
Discovery Phase Question Types	**Topic:** Help create a focused and productive 6th-7th-8th grade middle school math teacher team	**Topic:** Bringing together a cohesive school board
	Participants: 11 people: 9 general education teachers, 2 special education teachers	**Participants:** 9 people: 7 school board members, 1 superintendent, 1 assistant superintendent
1. A past, personal story	1. Describe a person who has made a difference in your life or someone you admire. What qualities were most outstanding about this person?	1. Describe who or what initially attracted you to this school district? How did you feel, once elected?
2. An outstanding moment or high point experience within the organization story	2. Describe a high point experience you have had with your teacher team. What were you doing that made you proud to be a part of the team?	2. Describe a high point experience you have had as a board member. Who was involved? What strengths did you bring as a leader to this team? What makes you most proud to be a member of the school board?
3. What is valued story	3. What do you value most about this teacher team?	3. Describe a time when the board experienced shared leadership that was successful or performed at its absolute best. With whom and how was the leadership shared? How did that shared leadership create a stronger, better board? What do you value most about leading this district?
4. Three wishes story	4. Describe three wishes for your team, so they could perform at their best. What are they?	4. If you could have three wishes that could bring out the best in your school board's leadership capacity, what would they be?

Table 3.3 The four types of questions asked during the AI 4-D cycle discovery phase with Example Sets 3 and 4

Discovery (Roles)	Discovery Questions Example Set 3	Discovery Questions Example Set 4
Discovery Phase Question Types	**Topic:** Create a three-year strategic plan for a school district.	**Topic:** Establish the vision and a technology plan for each school and overall district.
	Participants: 100 people: comprised of staff, parents, community, business, & industry.	**Participants:** 50 people: 3–5 members per school approximately 35 people, plus 7–10 technology staff and administrators; 3–5 business and industry representatives.
1. A past, personal story	1. Describe your favorite teacher and share a story about him/her teacher. What were the qualities he/she possessed that helped make that person your favorite teacher?	1. Share a story how you felt after purchasing/receiving your first technology device (e.g., game console, computer, laptop, ipad, cell phone). Who was involved? How old were you? What was the first thing you did with the device? Where were you?
2. An outstanding moment or high point experience within the organization story	2. Describe an outstanding moment or experience that you have had with our district that made you most proud to be a part of the district. Who was involved? What was happening?	2. Describe how technology has influenced your life or share an outstanding experience where technologies have made a difference in your life.
3. What is valued story	3. What do you value most about being associated with this district?	3. What do you value most about leading this district, its students, and staff through this century?
4. Three wishes story	4. What three wishes do you have for the school district if anything were possible?	4. If anything were possible, what three wishes would you have for students using technologies in this district?

math teacher team/PLC to be more productive with meeting time, content alignment, and on improving student learning. The first question asks the 11 teachers to share a past, personal story, describing a person who had made a difference in their life or someone that they admire. The question acts as a prompt to help the math teachers as storytellers recall details and extensive descriptions inclusive of qualities that were most outstanding about the person who made a difference in their life or of someone they admired. Sometimes, it may be necessary to ask multiple questions under each type of question so the person telling the story provides rich descriptions or helps clarify the meaning of his or her experiences. The first type of question, in the AI 4-D cycle discovery phase is a more personal narrative that helps with relationship building within the group.

Example Set 2 contains a similar question that asks for a past, personal story in Table 3.2. The board of education members are asked to share what initially attracted them to the school district to be a servant of the community. Example Set 3 in Table 3.3 consists of a broad spectrum of people from the school and community and asks participants to describe their favorite teacher and what qualities were most outstanding about that person. Again, they are sharing a past, personal story and in this case, a common or shared experience with 100+ people involved in strategic planning for the district. Example Set 4 in Table 3.3 asks members of the technology team to share a story about their first technology device purchase or gift. Again, the first discovery question is centered around a past, personal story that is highly likely to be a common experience for people serving on a technology committee.

The second type of question in the discovery phase refers to an outstanding moment or high point experience within the organization and is typically, specific to the topic and group of participants such as in Example Set 1 in Table 3.2 where the question asks each person to describe a high point experience they have had with their middle school teacher team. Again, additional questions may be asked to draw more description such as detailing what you were doing that made you proud to be a part of that team, who was with you, or where were you.

Question 3 in the AI 4-D cycle discovery phase is centered around values and asks what you value most about your teacher team (Example Set 1 in Table 3.2) or what you value most about leading the district in the role of a school board member (Example Set 2 in Table 3.2). Values help others understand what is important to you—what matters; they are your beliefs or convictions. Values help guide our decisions and even our behaviors. Values to consider may include honesty, trust, respect, open communication, creativity, humility, empathy, as well as being adaptable, transparent, or reliable. Knowing what you value is an important part of the AI process since the AI 4-D cycle involves establishing core values, which, in turn helps in accomplishing a collectively co-constructed vision for achieving goals, committing to action plans, and actualizing the desired results as determined by the team.

The fourth type of question in the discovery phase asks participants to share three wishes that might help their teacher team, school, or district perform at their best. Example Set 1 in Table 3.2 asks teachers to share three wishes for their middle school math teacher team that might help them perform at their very best. Wishes help participants express their aspirations or to expand the possibilities for the team, school, or district.

Notice the way questions are asked in the Example Sets 1 and 2 in Table 3.2 and Example Sets 3 and 4 in Table 3.3. Facilitators using the AI change model phrase questions with strengths-based language. The effect of the questioning process focuses on strengths, assets, and wishes that helps build the positive core (that which is valued or is of priority), which becomes the basis for the rest of the AI 4-D cycle change process.

Table 3.2 shows two example sets of discovery questions used in the AI 4-D cycle, discovery phase.

Table 3.3 shows two additional example sets with different topics depicting the four types of questions (past, personal; outstanding moment; what is valued; and wishes) used in storytelling during the AI 4-D cycle discovery phase. Multiple questions may be grouped to help elicit richer descriptions in the storytelling process as portrayed in Example Set 4, question 1.

Best practices for sharing stories

The AI 4-D cycle discovery phase asks participants four types of questions centered around the topic or focus of inquiry that serve as prompts so stories can be shared. Stories are told either in one-to-one interviews or pairs. One person in the pair tells stories using the questions in the sets as noted in Tables 3.2 and 3.3, while the other person listens and takes notes. Then the roles are reversed.

Next, the pair joins four or five other pairs (a small group of 8–10 people) where the stories are shared with the small group. One person in the small group becomes the recorder and takes notes on a large chart paper. One person from the original pair becomes the storyteller sharing their partner's stories. Then roles are switched, so the other partner in the pair shares out to the small group telling the stories the partner shared earlier. The storytelling process helps participants acquire a visual as another describes the situation. They share who was involved, what was happening at the time, and how that experience became an outstanding or best moment. A recorder keeps notes on a large chart paper that is visually displayed.

The first part of the AI 4-D cycle discovery phase has included the paired interviews and the pairs have joined and shared with three to four other pairs creating a small group (8–10 people). The small group has heard each other's stories based on the four questions asked from four different scenarios as noted in Tables 3.2 and 3.3. The four questions included a past, personal story; a high point or outstanding experience, characteristics in others they value or what they value, and wishes for the future. The next step in the discovery phase is to identify themes based on the recorder's notes and map the positive core—the factors deemed as most important to the small group.

Identifying themes and mapping the positive core

The second part of the discovery phase asks the small groups (8–10 people) to examine the notes taken on the large chart paper and identify common themes and key factors that helped make the situation a best moment or an outstanding experience, what is valued, and wishes or desires for the future. Mapping the positive core is a collaborative effort of coming together, examining the large chart papers for what unites, identifying patterns, strengths, values, and other significant factors. A small group of 8–10 people collaboratively create lists that identify the common themes and key factors: What were the qualities that made the stories "high point" or "outstanding experiences", identifying when the team is performing at its best, determining what is valued, and forming images for a future from the wishes presented. Figure 3.2 illustrates some of the large chart papers where themes, characteristics valued in others, high points, and key factors have been identified.

Figure 3.2 is a collage of large chart papers co-created during the AI 4-D cycle where common themes have been identified. Photograph taken by author.

The small group (8–10 people) prepares their lists of themes and key factors on the large chart paper and then prioritizes narrowing the lists down to 3–5 of the most important themes or main factors that would be the ultimate or ideal for their middle school team as is the case with Example Set 1 in Table 3.2 or as portrayed in the other examples: the board of education to operate more optimally at the district level; the staff and community members creating a district three-year strategic plan; and those involved in the design of the school's technology plan, or the district technology plan. The prioritized list from each small group is posted around the room and shared with the whole group. Once all groups have reported, then every person is given a set of sticky/Avery dots (usually 3–5 dots) to place beside the themes that are most important to them as an individual, which they feel should be a part of the middle school math team, or as in the case with the other three example sets, for the board of education, those participating in the district-wide

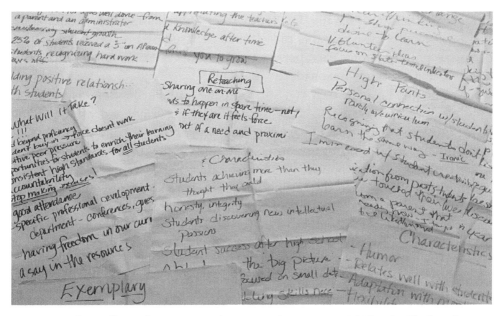

Figure 3.2 A collage of large chart papers with common themes created during the AI 4-D cycle.

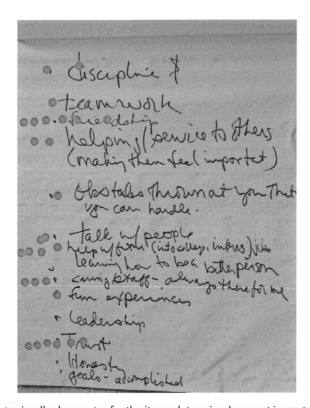

Figure 3.3 Sticky dots visually show votes for the items determined as most important to the group.

strategic planning, or for the development of the school/district technology plan. Individually, participants place the dots based on preference; this type of voting process allows each person to place dots on several lists or post all of them next to one theme or idea.

The themes or core factors with a greater number of dots as noted in Figure 3.2 serve as a visual to show what is most important and valued by the larger group. Keep in mind that each of the 3–5 themes listed and posted by the various small groups is important. The activities in the discovery phase serve as the basis for further capacity building in other phases in the AI 4-D cycle.

Figure 3.3 illustrates the voting process where sticky/Avery dots have been used to determine what is valued by individuals. In this case, friendship and trust were most important to the high school students participating in the 4-D cycle, discovery phase (San Martin, 2008). Photograph taken by author.

Discovery phase summary

The participants in the discovery phase interacted with one other person in paired interviews, sharing a past, personal story and an outstanding, positive experience. The pair shared their values and wishes for their school or district; the pair, then joined several other pairs creating a small group of 8–10 and shared each other's stories with other pairs. Intentionally, the goal is building relationships that help lay the groundwork for the next phases in the AI 4-D cycle. The hope is that a common bond may begin to form as they hear others' stories, ask clarifying questions, and reflect on what was shared. Typically, it is at this point that the small group begins to sense cohesiveness or even community as they co-construct common themes and create a prioritized list of what is most important and valued, the positive core.

Lastly, the small group shares the 3–5 most valued ideas listed that have been written on a large chart paper with the whole group. After sharing, the group posts their lists with the themes or factors deemed most important around the room. Each participant is given a set of 3–5 sticky dots and post their sticky dots next to themes listed on any group's chart paper. The dots visually show what is most valued or important to everyone in the room.

By the end of the discovery phase, the participants have connected with others through the stories and experiences shared. A visual, from the prioritized lists co-created by each small group, shows what is most valued among participants and the visual is even more pronounced with sticky dots clustered (Figure 3.3) around the most important factors or what is considered the positive core. The use of electronic devices such as classroom interactive white boards or phones using apps such as Poll Everywhere (n.d.) can be used for voting to help determine what is valued by individuals participating in the 4-D cycle as noted in Figures 3.4 and 3.5.

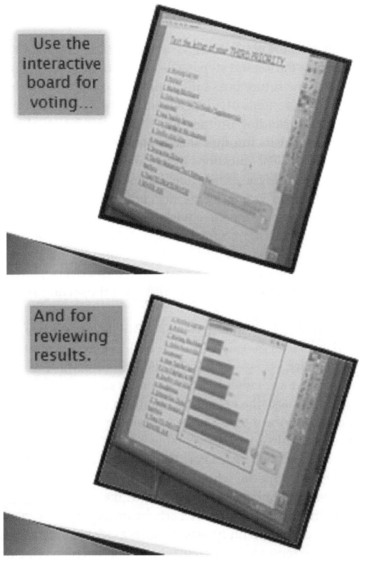

Figures 3.4 and 3.5 Depict how participants voted for their third priority via phone/clickers using an interactive board with instant group results noted in bar graph format.

Figures 3.4 and 3.5 show the priority voting process via an interactive board with the list and then results shown in a bar graph format.

The magic in storytelling is detected with the ongoing conversations and emotions exhibited by participants toward the end of the discovery phase. Enthusiasm builds, an inclusive bond develops among the participants, and an urge and openness to share subsequent stories exists among the conversations throughout the room. The next step in the AI 4-D cycle is the dream phase, where the groups have an opportunity to imagine the ideal future.

Step 2: Dream

Dream phase: imagine the possibilities

The dream phase is the second step in the AI 4-D cycle. The dream phase has two parts, to imagine future possibilities of what could be and then to begin to prioritize the components of an idealized future for the teacher teams, the school, or district depending on the topic of inquiry. The goal of the dream phase is vision consensus through shared stories of imagining the possibilities of what could be. The questions asked are stated in the affirmative and are the prompts for dialogue as noted in Tables 3.4 and 3.5. Stories shared are the delivery method to ignite energy and enthusiasm among participants. The dream phase considers the three wishes shared from the discovery phase, from the previous meeting. Using the same example sets topics 1–4 (e.g., Example Set 1, a more focused and productive middle school math teacher team) from the previous Tables 3.2 and 3.3 in the discovery phase, questions have now been created that could be used during the second step, the dream phase, of the AI 4-D cycle.

Table 3.4 contains Example Sets 1 and 2 with dream phase questions. Example Set 1 provides questions for the building administrator who facilitates the AI change process for the middle school math teacher team. The building administrator reviews the three wishes stated by the team from the discovery step, then asks the teachers to envision the team working together at their best and describe it as if it were happening in the present.

Question 1 in the dream phase in Table 3.4, asks the middle school math team to project a story, one year later. The scenario created in Example Set 1 in Table 3.4 stages the middle school math team as the recipient of the state's Mathematics Teaching Enhancement Award ($1,000 per teacher) for being the outstanding teaching team. The math teachers are asked to describe what they and their team are doing with questions such as, "What are you describing and showing to the reporters/TV crew who are observing your classrooms?"

Similar questions imagining future possibilities are asked in Example Set 2 in Table 3.4, where the goal of the educational leader is to help create a more cohesive school board. The school board members are asked individually to describe their vision for attaining the distinction of being the best school district in the nation. Then, they describe what the school district would look like on Friday morning if the impossible were possible. They are asked to tell the story as if they were giving the tours to visitors from across the nation. Detailed or descriptive questions are asked such as "What are we seeing? What are others doing? What makes us the best school district in the nation"? Extracting details is important so they can visualize the possibilities.

Table 3.4 The questions asked during the AI 4-D cycle dream phase with Example Sets 1 and 2

Dream (Possible Plays)	Dream Questions Example Set 1	Dream Questions Example Set 2
Dream Phase Questions	**Topic:** Help create a focused and productive 6th-7th-8th grade middle school math teacher team.	**Topic:** Bringing together a cohesive school board.
	Participants: 11 people: 9 general education teachers, 2 special education teachers.	**Participants:** 9 people: 7 school board members, 1 superintendent, 1 assistant superintendent.
1. Imagine future possibilities of what could be.	1. Review the three wishes that you had for your team from the Discovery phase. Add any additional thoughts to the list. Keeping those wishes in mind, envision your team working together at its best. What does that look like?	2. Describe your vision for attaining the distinction of being the best school district in the nation.
	2. One year has passed, and your middle school math team is the recipient of the state's Mathematics Teaching Enhancement Award ($2,000 per teacher) for outstanding teaching. Describe what you and your team are doing? What are you describing to the reporters/TV crew who are observing your classrooms that makes your team different?	2. Describe what your school district would look like on Friday morning if the impossible were possible. Tell the story as if each of you as school board members were giving the tours to visitors from across the nation. What are we seeing? What are others doing? What makes us the best school district in the nation?

Table 3.4 shows typical examples of the two questions asked during the AI 4-D cycle dream phase. One is a reflection question reviewing the wishes, which helps envision how the team might look when operating at their best; the other describes the wishes as if they had come true.

Table 3.5 shows the questions used in the AI 4-D cycle dream phase. The topics and participants remained the same as in Tables 3.2 and 3.3. The first action ask that participants review the three wishes from Tables 3.2 and 3.3

Table 3.5 The questions asked during the AI 4-D cycle dream phase with Example Sets 3 and 4

Dream (Possible Game Plays)	Dream Questions Example Set 3	Dream Questions Example Set 4
Dream Phase Questions	**Topic:** Create a three-year strategic plan for a school district.	**Topic:** Determine the vision and a technology plan for each school and overall district.
	Participants: 100 people: comprised of staff, parents, community, business, & industry.	**Participants:** 50 people: 3–5 members per school approximately 35 people, plus 7–10 technology staff and administrators; 3–5 business and industry representatives.
1. Imagine future possibilities of what could be.	1. What three wishes do you have for the school district? Dream big! Imagine the impossible becoming reality. 2. Three years have passed, and you have been invited back to celebrate the district's completed strategic plan. Now that you are on tour, describe what the district looks like and what is happening. Where are you? Who's involved?	1. Describe three wishes that you have for access to technology and the integration of technology throughout the district. 2. Wave your magic wand and describe what the district looks like and what is happening if the impossible were possible tomorrow. Describe what every classroom looks like and how they are different. Tell what technologies are used to support student learning. Imagine how students learn. What are they doing? What tools are available?

from the discovery phase, and then in Tables 3.4 and 3.5, participants are asked to imagine the wishes have come true.

The middle school math teacher team in the Example Set 1 in Table 3.4 identifies the themes from what each member says is happening and how they are describing the teacher team as working together and functioning. One option, to help visualize the imagined future, is to review results through wish or dream statements (e.g., create a video, act out a skit, draw a mural, write a story/poem, song, use a metaphor) before writing vision statements. The middle school math teachers could capture the dream by physically acting out a TV news report. They could work together to create the scene where a couple of the teachers play the role of the news reporter and camera-man who are observing what is happening in the classroom. The others are the math teachers being interviewed in their classrooms, describing what is happening and what is different, addressing how their teacher team is performing more collaboratively, improving student learning via coordinated, relevant projects.

Once the teacher team has acted out the scenario, they move to the second part of the dream phase, which is to discuss and analyze the acting that had just occurred. They determine what could be possible by listing most common phrases on a big chart paper, reviewing the data for success factors, and voting (using the sticky dots) on the actions most valued by the individual math teachers in the team. Alternatives to voting (e.g., three dots to each person) are to create the lists on an interactive board and vote with clickers or create and display votes through live polls through their phones as noted in Figures 3.4 and 3.5. Lastly, the facilitator or building administrator then asks the teacher team to prioritize the top three to five themes most valued; typically, the priority is focused on those with the most dots as pictured in Figure 3.3. The next step is to move to the design phase of the AI 4-D cycle process to create bold, vision statements of an idealized future for the school's teacher team, or in the case of Example Sets 2, 3, and 4, the district or school levels.

Dream phase summary

The dream phase is the second step of the 4-D cycle. Example Set 1 (Table 3.4) had the middle school math teachers review the three wishes they listed for their team from the discovery phase. Keeping those wishes in mind, they were asked in the dream phase to envision their teacher team working together at its best. They discussed the possibilities. They acted visually, illustrating what their team could look like by fast forwarding a year and using the scenario of their teacher team being a recipient of an excellence in teaching award. Once the teacher team had acted out the scenario, the teachers were asked to write down their descriptions of what happened. Three other sets of examples were provided in Tables 3.4 and 3.5. Acting out and imagining the ideal future where their wishes have come true helps set the background for writing the vision statements, which is the goal for Step 3, the design phase.

Step 3: Design

Design phase: create the future

The design phase is the third step in the AI 4-D cycle. The goal is to transform the vision into practical application. That is, describe the change or innovation: Creating the ideal middle school math teacher team, a cohesive board of education, a school-wide technology vision that aligns with the district's technology plan, or a district-wide strategic plan. The prioritized lists which contained the most important factors, known as the positive core, from both the discovery and dream phases are reviewed in the design phase. The participants in the design phase create bold, statements (provocative propositions) of an idealized future merging the best of what was valued and seen as strengths from the discovery phase with the vision for the ideal future from the dream phase.

The images from the scenario in the dream phase that were acted out by the middle school teacher team example, help in writing the bold, vision statements. Rather than acting out a scene like the middle school math teacher team, the participants could create metaphors, songs, or poems to help visualize the future, which can be referenced to help in creating the vision statements. It is important to remember the topic for change or innovation and how that aligns with the priorities and values established in the discovery and dream phases.

The work previously completed, the experiences, and relationships developed in the discovery and dream phases are used to create the bridge for the design and destiny phases in the AI 4-D cycle. The best from the past, the valued characteristics, and most important factors (e.g., values, strengths, wishes) identified from the discovery phase and the dream phases are used in the design phase to create the bold, vision statements. The main question in the design phase asks, what would our teacher team, school, or district look like if it were designed using all the important factors from the lists created in the discovery and dream phases?

The bold, vision statements describe the most important factors from both the discovery phase and the dream phase. The set of bold, vision statements typically address four priority points:

people (who we are and who are we when we are at our best),
purpose (our goal),
principles (what we value and believe), and
practices (the world we want to live in and create together as a teacher team).

The four priority points are focused on the topic of change or innovation. The vision statements are flexible and should address what was identified in the discovery and dream phases as being the most important factors or elements to the topic. That may mean addressing roles, relationships, and partnerships; management and policy; program coherence, resources, and data-driven results; or developing leadership skills/capacity through behaviors such as trust, respect, commitment, shared decision-making, compassion, inclusivity, and equity in addressing school climate and culture.

The bold, vision statements in the design phase define what allows the dream to become a reality. The final set of vision statements should reflect the team's shared vision, the preferred future. The vision statements should be written in the present tense as if the future were happening in the present moment. The middle school math teacher team would address the four priority points: People, purpose, principles, and practices by completing sentences such as "The middle school math teacher team values….our purpose or goal is… and we purposely or consciously….we believe….we commit to …we make a collaborative effort to practice…". The team's completion of the sentences help create the bold, vision statements. When completed, the vision statements should challenge the status quo.

The participants write bold, vision statements that incorporate the most important factors from the prioritized lists to help realize the dream. The Example Set 1, the middle school teacher team, had 11 members, so they worked in pairs (four groups of 2 and one group of 3). Example Set 2, the school board and administrative team, in Table 3.4 had nine participants, so they could work in pairs with three groups of 2 and one group of 3, or three groups of 3 to create vision statements. The pair or groupings of three share with another pair, have dialogue over the two sets of bold, vision statements, and then merge into one set of statements. Then the combined set of vision statements are shared with the whole group. The whole group then take the last two sets of vision statements remaining and merge into one final set of vision statements.

The Example Sets 3 and 4 in Table 3.5 are much larger groups. Example Set 3 has 100 people involved in the district strategic planning process, and Example Set 4 has 50 people involved in creating/renewing a district-wide technology plan. With larger numbers of participants, the process of writing bold, vision statements is easier if table groups of 8–10 people form as one group. Each table group of 8–10 people creates their bold, vision statements addressing the four priority points: People, purpose, principles, and practices. Once created, then each table group of 8–10 people joins another table group for an approximate number of 16–20 people. The two table groups share their sets of bold, vision statements.

After the two table groups (16–20 people) compare both groups' vision statements, they merge or integrate the two sets of statements into one set of vision statements. In the design phase, the bold, vision statements created by each table group will need to be narrowed down to one actual operating set of vision statements. The final set of vision statements created in the design phase provide a clear, result-oriented vision that exhibits the potential of the team, school, or district topic.

A common process for narrowing the vision statements down to one set is to operate much like using a 16- or 8-single elimination bracket, depending on the whole group size as seen in Figure 3.6. Each table group completes their vision statement. If there are 16 table groups of 8–10 people, then the 16 table groups pair with another table, so the total numbers of groups are reduced to eight. The eight groups are reduced to four groups and then two groups. Once there are two groups, then the whole group works together to construct the final vision statements that describe the vision for the ideal way of operating. This process is also used at the beginning of an AI 4-D cycle process when establishing the team norms or ground rules. The final co-constructed vision statements that create the future, then lead to the fourth and final phase in the AI 4-D cycle, the destiny phase.

Figure 3.6 is a 16-team single elimination bracket sample that has table groups labeled on the chart, showing how to narrow the multiple groups until there is one final set of team norms /ground rules or vision statements co-constructed to be posted and followed. Bracket from Printzdotorg (n.d.) and labeled by the author.

Design phase summary

Participants in the third step of the 4-D cycle, the design phase, capture the dream by creating a bold, vision statement (provocative proposition) that addresses the values and priorities from the discovery and dream phases. Example Set 1, where the goal is to have a more focused and productive middle school math team, stated wishes for their teacher team in the discovery phase. Next, they created visual images by acting out a scenario for a preferred future for the teacher team from the dream phase. Both the wishes and visual images for a preferred future were used to create the vision statement in the design phase, which defines who they are when they are at their best, their purpose, what they believe, and the world they want to co-create.

Figure 3.6 A 16-team single elimination bracket sample with 16 table groups (8–10 people per table) labeled on the chart.

Once the vision statement had been created, then the Example Set 1, middle school math teacher team, must ask if the components in the vision statement describe what the team wants as the preferred future—their purpose and intent. Revisions are allowed, then once finalized, the educational leader, as facilitator for the AI 4-D change process, guides the middle school teacher team to Step 4, the destiny phase, where the teachers begin to realize the dream by translating the vision statement into goals, strategies, and action items.

Step 4: Destiny

Destiny phase: making it happen—the game plan
The destiny phase is the fourth step in the AI 4-D cycle. The destiny phase is action planning where the participants develop the tasks and steps necessary to making the shared, co-constructed vision statements happen. The original

mastermind and creator of AI, David Cooperrider, believes "we create the organizational worlds we live in" (Cooperrider et al., 2003, p. 326). The goal in the destiny phase is to create a different world that the participants want to live in—the world they have envisioned for their middle school math teacher team, for their school and district's technology plan, for the operation of a more cohesive board of education at the district level, or a district-wide, three-year strategic plan. The agreed upon set of bold, vision statements is posted, and the conversations revolve around what it will take to make each statement a reality. The question asked in the destiny phase is, what will it take to make the dream happen or come true?

The destiny phase engages participants in conversations creating the actions necessary to make the dream come true. This involves collective focus and collaborative effort. The task is to create an action or implementation plan similar to the template provided in Table 3.6. The priorities developed in the dream and design phases and the vision statements are addressed in the action plan template. Conversations are held by each of the table groups where the first priority is discussed. The focus is in answering, what will it take to make that dream or priority happen. The table groups work together to complete the action plan. Table 3.6 is a template used to create the action plan, detailing what the participants believe the tasks and necessary steps should be to make the first or top priority a reality. Completed action plans are located in the scenario examples, Chapters 5–8 of this book.

Table 3.6 is an action plan template. When completed, it addresses, "what will it take to make the dream a happen?" Priorities co-constructed in the dream and design phases are listed along with the tasks and steps necessary to make the priority a reality. The discussions that occur answer the 4Ws + 2Hs: Who, What, Where, When, plus How and How much.

A detailed plan is co-constructed, outlining the steps that need to be taken along with timelines and celebration milestones. The plan should answer the 4Ws + 2Hs: Who, What, Where, When, plus How and How much. The excitement builds as participants operationalize the action plan defining the tasks involved, listing the activities that need to be completed, writing goals, and determining deadlines. Their engagement in the process yields a sense of how they can contribute personally to achieving the overall dream. Personal commitment to tasks or actions take the form of a self-organized activity. The energy and focus created from participation in the AI 4-D process produces a desire or hunger to continue involvement in the change projects and initiatives that comprise the action plan.

Table 3.6 A template for creating the action plan

Action Plan: Topic							
Objective/Goal:							
Current Situation:							
Priority 1:							
Task 1:							
What (Action Step Description)	Who (Person/Dept Responsible)	When (Begin Date)	When (Due Date)	How (Materials/ resources needed)	How much (Costs)	Notes
Step 1						
Step 2						
Step 3						
Task 2:							
What (Action Step Description)	Who (Person/Dept Responsible)	When (Begin Date)	When (Due Date)	How (Materials/ resources needed)	How much (Costs)	Notes
Step 1						
Step 2						

Destiny phase summary

Participants in the fourth and last step of the 4-D cycle, the destiny phase, co-construct an action plan based on the vision statements created in the design phase. The action plan operationalizes the vision statements and becomes the visual or game plan so progress can be monitored, reviewed, and reprioritized that lead to the vision, the realization of their preferred future. The 4Ws + 2Hs: Who, What, Where, When, plus How and How much are addressed in the action planning process. Participants are asked to commit to some part of the action plan. Participants leave the destiny phase of the AI 4-D cycle with the game plan or playbook—the action plan and their personal commitments to turning the plans into their new, desired world. Chapter 4 prepares educational leaders for game day.

Summary: Chapter 3 how to facilitate change using the AI 4-D cycle

Participation in the 4Ds: Discovery, Dream, Design, and Destiny phases are likened to the roles, plays, game plans that make up a coach's playbook.
First step: Determine the topic—the focus for change, written in the affirmative. Four examples used throughout the chapter were to….

- help create a focused and productive 6–8 grade middle school math teacher team (11 participants).
- develop a more cohesive school board (nine participants).
- create a three-year strategic plan for a school district (100 participants).
- determine the vision and a technology plan for each school and overall district (50 participants).

Second step: How the AI 4-D cycle works:

- Phase 1 Discovery: Share stories and identify themes (what made those past experiences outstanding) and begin to map the positive core by sharing what's most valued or the core beliefs, best practices, and strengths.
- Phase 2 Dream: Imagine future possibilities of what could be and prioritize, gaining consensus of what should be the idealized future.
- Phase 3 Design: Create bold, vision statements (provocative propositions) of an idealized future. Prioritize and gain consensus of what should be.
- Phase 4 Destiny: Commit to the co-created action plan and to sustaining the plan, making it happen!

References

Cooperrider, D. L., Whitney, D., & Stavros, J. M. (2003). *Appreciative inquiry handbook: The first in a series of AI workbooks for leaders of change* (1st ed.). Lakeshore.

Fine, S. (2022). Lead the change series: Q & A with Sara Fine. *AERA Educational Change Special Interest Group, 128*, 1–4. http://www.aera.net/SIG155/Lead-the-Change-Series

Polk, R. (1982). *Baseball playbook*. University Press of Mississippi.

Poll Everywhere. (n.d.). *Instant poll voting on smartphones*. Retrieved August 13, 2022, from https://www.polleverywhere.com/smartphone-web-voting

Printzdotorg. (n.d.). Sports single elimination bracket. *Printzdotorg*. Retrieved August 11, 2022, from https://printz.org/Sports/Single-Elimination-Bracket/

San Martin, T. L. (2008). *Empowering students to enhance pedagogy: An apprecia-tive inquiry case study of alternative high school students' high point learning experiences* [Dissertation, Wichita State University]. Wichita State Univer-sity SOAR. https://soar.wichita.edu/handle/10057/1956

Self, B. (2020). *Bill Self's offensive playbook*. Championship Productions. https://www.championshipproductions.com/cgi-bin/champ/p/Basketball/Bill-Selfs-Offensive-Playbook_BD-05696A.html?mv_form_charset=ut-f%2d8%26%230%3butf%2d8&mv_session_id=PtfDbbKkvHnb&id=PtfDbbKkvHnb

4

Preparing for gameday

How do football teams prepare for the Super Bowl or how do middle school volleyball teams prepare for a match? Behind the scenes preparations are necessary that include both planning ahead for the event and management of the event itself. Typically, a meeting is held to address what is about to happen with a discussion on the preparation needed, and then the coach works through mindset strategies to help players stay focused. When educational leaders plan for an event, whether it be a staff meeting or a district-wide, back-to-school event, behind the scenes preparations include meetings similar to those preparing for the gameday of the Superbowl. Someone needs to determine goals of the event, who attends, how many will be attending, when and where the event will be held. Decisions need to be made regarding the schedule and speakers, facilitators, sponsors, caterers, equipment acquisition, and infrastructural needs, plus the development of a communication plan for the attendees. Someone is responsible for planning and preparations that are critical to the success of each meeting or event, much like a team's preparation with practices and trainings that lead up to gameday.

The appreciative inquiry (AI) change model includes a 4-D cycle or process that can be a one-time event held over multiple days for the whole educational community such as in the case of a district-wide strategic planning event with hundreds of attendees. The event could be 40 staff members from one middle school held at the school location for two mornings; it could be a one-time event involving all district employees, or monthly, regularly scheduled administrator meetings, or grade level teacher team meetings.

DOI: 10.4324/9781003350804-4

A commonly used term when using the AI 4-D cycle is the word, summit. An AI summit refers to a large (many times 100s of people) and diverse gathering of stakeholders who participate in the AI 4-D cycle consisting of meetings usually held over a two- to three-day period, focused on development of the organization where participants create a shared vision and future for employees and customers (Ludema et al., 2003).

Due to the flexibility with the AI change model, the 4-D step process may be cyclical and repetitive in nature with grade level team/department meetings scheduled on a regular basis such as weekly or monthly where the groups continue working through the four steps. The AI 4-D cycle, when completed, repeats as the focus or topic changes.

One such example of an iteration occurred when the school superintendent focused on the topic of developing strong leadership skills among the district's administrative team with the purpose of helping the building level administrators become collaborative leaders. The superintendent facilitated the AI 4-D change process. She guided the administrative team through the 4Ds which helped bring clarity to the district's mission, what was valued by the administrative team while simultaneously building relationships and trust among the group. Throughout the AI process over multiple meetings, the administrative team seemed to be more open to others' ideas and assessing their own effectiveness as a leader with action planning goals of becoming more active listeners and resolving conflict in constructive, collaborative ways.

One of the top priority action planning goals with the administrative leadership team was learning how to resolve conflict in more constructive, collaborative ways. The district administrative team mapped out the AI 4-D cycle using a similar template found in Chapter 9. With confidence, the building administrators used the AI 4-D cycle engaging staff in their buildings through the change process to help promote a more welcoming and positive school climate, which in turn had a trickle-down effect into the classroom level, moving toward expectations where staff developed inviting classroom environments and established behavioral and academic standards while encouraging each other with ways to help students develop social and emotional learning skills. Once the team or group becomes familiar with the AI 4-D change process, then iteration involves the repetition of steps by the cyclical nature as noted in Figure 3.1 in Chapter 3. The AI 4-D process becomes easier and more natural with practice.

Having a lead person as facilitator is valuable to the AI process while getting started and learning the 4-D steps in the cycle. The facilitator needs to be familiar with AI as a way of thinking where questions used in the process are worded using strengths-based language (in a positive versus negative manner) and then in understanding the four steps involved in the change method, known as the AI 4-D cycle. Both, understanding the way questions are framed and learning the four steps in the AI 4-D process, can be learned by studying the playbook scenarios that follow in Chapters 5–8. The role of the facilitator and who to consider as the facilitator is discussed, along with a "how to get started" descriptive process for establishing team norms or ground rules.

The facilitator's role

The facilitator may be involved with reserving and setting up the meeting facilities, acquisition of event materials, setting and pacing the agenda, and other logistics such as access to technologies or determining meals, snacks, or refreshments. The role of the facilitator(s) is important when you have an event with large numbers of attendees. The facilitator has multiple tasks, managing small groups and pairing groups as they become larger and larger. An example was shown in Figure 3.6, where there were 16 tables with 8–10 people per table. Also, the Playbook Scenarios in Part II of this book provide examples of various sized AI events. Playbook Scenario 1 example (Chapter 5, Table 5.1) has approximately 130 staff and administrators participating in the AI 4-D cycle, so it may be advantageous to have co-facilitators (2–3 people) for larger groups who can help with posting large chart papers, helping to pair table groups, and assisting with movement around the room.

The facilitator has multiple responsibilities when the organization or school district has invested time and money in having 130 employees participate in a typical two or three-day appreciative inquiry 4-D change process ranging from preparation and coordination of the event to implementation of the AI change process. The facilitator reserves the meeting room(s) and ensures all technical equipment and supplies are available. Supplies typically include large chart paper and butcher paper that can be visibly displayed, tape, markers, and colored sticky dots for voting. Computers capable of projecting visuals on a wall with voting software such as Poll Everywhere (n.d.) can also be used as noted in Chapter 3, Figures 3.4 and 3.5.

The facilitator acts as the leader, guiding participants through the change process. The facilitator has advanced knowledge of the purpose and goals for the meetings and is comfortable with the AI process. The facilitator creates and reviews the agenda with the group. The facilitator helps keep people focused, following the agenda, and is the timekeeper. This person helps the group establish the team norms or ground rules, and then reminds the group from time to time the agreed upon team norms or ground rules. Facilitators prepare the guiding questions to be used in the AI 4-D cycle: Discovery, Dream, Design, and Destiny that open the discussions.

From time to time, the facilitator may ask participants to form smaller groups and then report to larger groups creating a balance in participation. The smaller groups may be asked to self-manage their group with assigned roles such as recorder, reporter, or timekeeper, who then report to the larger groups. The facilitator captures the main ideas, actions, and decisions made by the participants, and summarizes the notes with the groups clarifying and getting confirmation of understanding throughout the meetings. The facilitator also provides closure to the meetings by reviewing accomplishments for the day and then distributes the summarized notes that were confirmed by the group. The facilitator does not make decisions.

Who should be facilitator?

The facilitator should have a good understanding of how the four steps flow in the AI 4-D cycle change process. The facilitator does not have the answers, nor does this person tell the participants what decisions to make. The facilitator position does not have to be a person who has a direct relationship to the meetings or goals to be accomplished by those participating in the AI 4-D cycle. The facilitator should understand the purpose and goals that the group is trying to accomplish.

The topic in Chapter 5, Playbook Scenario 1 is teacher retention. The facilitator could be the Assistant Superintendent for Curriculum and Instruction who is not directly involved with the issue or with the five participating schools, which is the case in the Playbook Scenario 1. The facilitator could be a person who is directly involved, such as one of the five building principals or two of the teachers as co-facilitators. Studying the example playbook scenarios provided in the next few chapters will provide a clearer picture with further details to help gain an understanding of the AI 4-D cycle process as well as the way of thinking, based on the questions being asked throughout each of the 4-Ds.

The facilitator in the Playbook Scenario 3 in Chapter 7 is the high school English department head/PLC lead teacher who has a supplemental contract. The lead teacher gets paid to plan and facilitate the weekly or monthly meetings as designated by the school's administration. She is directly responsible for the meetings with the 14 general education English teachers and the two special education teachers. The English department head, as facilitator, uses the AI 4-D cycle as the change process to accomplish the goals of culti-vating a shared sense of purpose, leading the department's curriculum devel-opment, content alignment, and classroom and state assessment expectations ensuring a focus on improving student learning, as well as allotting time for teachers to reflect and improve classroom practices.

Among other duties, the person designated as facilitator helps foster a culture of collegiality and healthy team dynamics. The underlying principles (Cooperrider et al., 2008) that AI is built upon, bringing the best from the past and what works via shared stories of success and imagining what could be, using strengths-based language, and applying the 4-D cycle as the process or methodology provide the ideal framework necessary for fostering a positive climate and culture of inclusivity. The more frequently the AI 4-D cycle is used as the preferred method for change, the easier the process becomes, and since it is iterative in nature, knowing the 4Ds expedites the change needed in an already rapidly changing environment. The facilitator is also instrumental in guiding the process for establishing ground rules or team norms.

Getting started: establishing ground rules or team norms

Once the topic or focus has been established and the players or participants have been identified, the facilitator helps participants establish the norms or ground rules as the first step in the meeting process. The facilitator introduces the topic or focus for the meeting, the change process known as AI with its 4-D cycle, and then reviews the agenda for the meeting. The participants establish the ground rules or norms that the groups agree to live by when meeting. The ground rules are agreed upon by the overall group and are posted on large chart paper to be visually available during meetings.

In a large gathering, with 130 people as in the Playbook Scenario 1 example (Chapter 5), it becomes necessary to start with table groups of 8–9 people who create a brainstormed list of team norms or ground rules at each table. The process for establishing team norms or ground rules for large groups is much like the 16-team single elimination brackets as noted in Chapter 3 (Figure 3.6) when working through the 4D process in the AI 4-D cycle. The sixteen tables or groups complete a set of team norms or ground rules. Then each table group pairs up with another table group. They share their set of team norms or ground rules with each other. The pair of table groups come to consensus, merging the two table sets into one new set of team norms or ground rules. Now there are eight sets. The process continues until there are four sets and then two sets of team norms or ground rules. Participants go back to their original table groups while the final two sets of team norms or ground rules are posted. Participants review and combine the last two remaining sets into one set of team norms or ground rules for the whole group to follow.

The team norms or ground rules remain posted throughout the AI summit or meetings as a visual reminder. The facilitator may have to remind the group from time to time to follow the agreed upon rules. If rules are frequently violated, the facilitator may suggest that the agreed upon team norms or ground rules be changed. The process then repeats itself.

Creating the team norms or ground rules can be accomplished in a couple of ways with smaller groups, depending on the size of the group. The facilitator, in the Playbook Scenario 3, (Chapter 6) with 16 teachers from the high school English department, can place the large chart paper on an easel and go around the room clockwise and have one person at a time add a team norm or ground rule to the chart paper with the option of passing. Another way is to divide the 16-teacher team into two groups of eight and have each group brainstorm a list, then post the two lists, compare for similarities and differences, and through discussion co-construct a final set of norms that are agreed upon by the whole group.

The ground rules may be revised at any time so long as the rules are agreed upon by the group; again, it is important that ground rules or team norms are visually displayed and reviewed before each meeting. Table 4.1 provides two examples of team norms or ground rules. The Playbook Scenario 1

Table 4.1 Two examples of team norms or ground rules

Norms/Ground Rules	Meeting Manifesto (Rules We Agreed On)
Food!!	Limit use of devices
Be positive	Come prepared—bring examples (evidence)
Be on time/stay until the end of the meeting	Start on time
Be open-minded	Stay on task—comments and tasks must be related
Be honest and respectful	All participate; all share responsibility
Work with each other—make an effort	Be respectful and optimistic
Be present—no screen time	Agree on tasks for the next meeting before adjournment or leaving!

(Chapter 5) focused on teacher retention was created with approximately 130 staff and administrators on the left side. The team norms or ground rules for the Playbook Scenario 3 example (Chapter 7), the 16 high school English teachers that form a department or PLC, are displayed on the right-hand side of Table 4.1 as a Meeting Manifesto. Writing the task or goal for the meeting may also be added or posted visually so participants have the visuals in front of them as a constant reminder.

Table 4.1 depicts two example sets of team norms or ground rules which were agreed upon by participants. Team norms or ground rules are to be displayed always, reviewed prior to each meeting, enforced by the facilitator, and revised as needed throughout the AI 4-D cycle process.

The next step is to help the facilitator begin the discovery phase of the AI 4-D cycle. The "how" to create change is presented in the form of playbooks with scenarios or examples that walk you through the AI 4-D cycle. The playbook is likened to a set of instructions (the plays) centered on a topic where participants want change, innovation, or a task completed. The example scenarios or playbooks, using the AI 4-D cycle, will help guide educational leaders through the decision-making process so change becomes a preferred routine method that is participatory, inclusive, and successful for participants.

Playbooks as scenario examples

The playbooks are example scenarios. They are stories with a purpose that detail the AI steps used in the 4-D cycle: Discovery, Dream, Design, and Destiny. The playbooks or scenario examples contain questions used within the 4-D cycle that are aligned to the AI philosophy, worded using strengths-based language. Each scenario is based on an educational issue and how the participants chose to address that issue changing their future for their school or district. Selected responses made by participants involved in the AI change process are provided.

Chapters 5–8 contain a playbook with a different scenario that visually displays the steps taken in the AI 4-D process to ensure change happens. The scenarios are set up in the same format for each chapter. The discovery phase asks people to work in pairs and answer four initial questions: a past, personal story; high point, outstanding experiences; characteristics in others they value or what they value; and wishes for the future. The dream phase asks participants to take the best of the past or current situation and wishes from the discovery phase and imagine future possibilities for their situations. The design phase asks participants to create bold, vision statements defining who they are and where they want to be based on the imagined future in the dream phase. The destiny phase is the action and commitment to realizing the future. The decisions made by the participants in the design and destiny phases involve the collaborative efforts from the whole group where all views, voices, and diversities have been heard and considered throughout the AI experience. The destiny phase is completed in the form of an action plan providing details of what is to be accomplished, who is to be held accountable with deadlines, and resources needed.

The playbooks, as scenarios, in Chapters 5–8, offer concrete educational contexts, both situational and organizational, for learning and studying the AI 4-D cycle. Each chapter provides a scenario, a different story that purposefully addresses a relevant educational challenge. The four phases in the AI 4-D cycle remain the same, however, the guiding questions change based on the purpose, the focus or topic of inquiry, as noted in the title of each chapter. The details provided in each scenario will help bring clarity to the AI 4-D cycle change method. Each chapter concludes with a summary of the AI 4-D process, detailing the logistics, and providing a follow up on sustaining the plan. Reviewing each scenario will help prepare you as the educational leader to be facilitator ready to lead change in your building or district.

The facilitator has prepared for gameday and is now ready to coach the game.

Summary: Chapter 4 preparing for Gameday

The AI 4-D cycle can be a district-wide, one-time event for 2–3 days or can be used in weekly, biweekly, or monthly administrator or teacher team/PLC meetings.

The role of the facilitator, you as the educational leader, includes:

- securing the meeting facilities, technical equipment, supplies, food/ snacks.
- knowing the purpose of the meeting(s) or AI summit.
- preparing the agenda and guiding questions on the topic.
- guiding the group/participants as they establish the team norms or ground rules.
- monitoring the meeting(s) and being the timekeeper, keeping participants focused while guiding participants through the change process, and summarizing notes confirmed by the group.

The facilitator does not have the answers, nor do they make decisions.

Who should be the facilitator? The facilitator should…
- be an educational leader or team member.
- consider having co-facilitators based on group size.
- be someone familiar with the AI process and the 4-D cycle.

Scenarios are written in playbook format. The scenarios…
- offer concrete educational examples with change solutions.
- include the play-by-play steps using the AI 4-D cycle to bring change and make shared decisions.
- provide participant guiding questions, a sampling of responses, action plans, and a summary of each scenario.

Details are found in Chapters 5–8.

References

Cooperrider, D. L., Whitney, D., Stavros, J. M., & Fry, R. (2008). *The appreciative inquiry Handbook: For leaders of change.* Crown Custom.

Ludema, J. D., Whitney, D., Mohr, B. J., & Griffin, T. J. (2003). *The appreciative inquiry summit: A practitioner's guide for leading large-group change.* Berrett-Koehler.

Poll Everywhere. (n.d.). Instant poll voting on smartphones. Retrieved August 13, 2022, from https://www.polleverywhere.com/smartphone-web-voting.

5

Playbook for Scenario 1—increasing teacher retention

Topic or focus of inquiry—how can our district increase teacher retention at the elementary level?

This chapter, the Playbook for Scenario 1, focuses on the topic of teacher retention where teacher attrition and turnover has been an issue for the school district at the elementary level. The chapter includes descriptions for the appreciative inquiry (AI) 4-D cycle. Sample questions used to guide discussions along with selected responses made by participants are included in the chapter tables. The 4-D steps are noted first, then the co-created action plan, a summary of the process, and a follow up on sustaining the plan are included.

The roles of those in the Scenario 1 example included the elementary staff from five elementary buildings within the school district, their building principals, and the school district superintendent. Also invited were district personnel who had an interest in teacher retention such as the human resources director, the communications director, and the district level assistant superintendents.

The playbook for the Scenario 1 example asks, how can our district increase teacher retention at the elementary level? The AI meetings were designed as a large setting for approximately 130 people participating with a facilitator and two others, as co-facilitators, to help with group logistics. In this case, the facilitator was the district's assistant superintendent with two building administrators assisting. The two-day event took place in one of the

DOI: 10.4324/9781003350804-5

elementary multipurpose rooms, but it could occur in a large, multipurpose room such as a middle school lunchroom area or hotel conference or ballroom that accommodates 120–130 people with 8–10 people per round table. A sample two-day agenda can be found in Chapter 9. Table 5.1 provides the details for the AI 4-D cycle discovery phase, which includes the guiding questions and a selection of responses. Tables 5.2–5.4 provide the details for the dream, design, and destiny phases. Table 5.5 shows the action plan that includes the overall objective, priorities, goals, tasks, timelines, and responsible parties.

The AI 4-D cycle

Table 5.1 shows the topic, teacher retention, with approximately 130 participants involved in the AI 4-D cycle discovery phase. A sample of guiding questions and several responses are provided as participants shared stories (the best from the past) to help the group discover strengths, values, and wishes for their elementary buildings and the district. The second part of the discovery phase asked participants to identify the themes from what was shared and determine what was most valued by the group, and to identify best practices and strengths.

Table 5.2 shows the questions used in the second step of the AI 4-D cycle, known as the dream phase. Like the discovery phase, there are two parts. Part A asks participants to imagine future possibilities of what could be—related to the topic of teacher retention. Specifically, participants were asked, if the impossible were possible, what three wishes would you have so teachers would be lined up to work in the #1 rated district in the state and the other questions project their wishes into the future as if their wishes had come true three years later. Samples of participant responses are given.

Part B has participants reviewing the data so themes can be identified. The same process for reviewing data is used throughout the AI 4-D cycle whether participants are establishing group norms and ground rules or reviewing shared table data and can be found under the heading Agenda later in Chapter 9 or reviewed as part of the facilitator role with a depiction of table groupings in Figure 3.6 in Chapter 3. Participants' Priority 1 was to promote a positive image of the district, and Priority 2 was to increase principal leadership capacity.

Table 5.3 guides the 130 elementary principals and staff through the design phase. The results from the first two phases, discovery and dream, are used to create the design phase where bold, vision statements of the future are

Table 5.1 Teacher retention: the AI 4-D cycle discovery phase

Background	Description	Sample Questions used to Guide the 4-D Cycle	Sample Responses
Topic	Area of focus for change, innovation:	How can our district increase teacher retention at the elementary level?	
Participants	Who needs to be involved in the change process?	• Certified staff at the five elementary schools. • Building principals. • District personnel such as superintendents and directors of human resources and special education services. • 2–3 people who serve as co-facilitators.	• Five elementary schools with licensed staff who had been employed by the district for at least one year were invited (119 eligible teachers/special education teachers, librarians, counselors). • 5 principals, 2 assistant principals. • 1 HR director, 1 director of elementary student services, 1 superintendent, 1 director of special education services. Total: 130 participants.

Step 1 in the AI 4-D Cycle: Discovery

Step	Description	Sample Questions used to Guide the 4-D Cycle	Sample Responses
1. Discovery (Roles)	Part A. Share stories (the best from the past) to discover strengths, values, and wishes.	What most attracted you to this district or the school where you work?	**Attraction:** • Smaller community, near the city for shopping. • Friendliness. • Willingness to help the new person. • More athletic opportunities for my kids.

(continued)

Background	Description	Sample Questions used to Guide the 4-D Cycle	Sample Responses
		Describe a high point experience where you were most proud to be an employee in the X School District. Who was involved? What was happening?	**High Point Experience in District:** • After being treated in such a positive way with my children attending three different schools in the district, I decided to return to teaching at the encouragement of some of the current teachers and what they had to say about their jobs/job satisfaction in this district. • Recognized at a school board meeting for having a positive attitude; felt appreciated and supported. • Being assigned a mentor for the first two years who helped with the technology, the online teaching options, grading, instructional materials available, etc…it seemed so overwhelming at first.
	Share stories (the best from the past) to discover strengths, values, and wishes.	Describe a high point experience where you were most proud to be a staff member at X Elementary School? Who was involved? What was happening?	**High Point Experience at Building Level:** • Proud of X and our school for having the "Teacher of the Year" for the county. • We had a principal who valued our ideas and let us implement a recess/lunch time health fitness walk program with student awards (e.g., pedometers for 5th graders) for reaching milestones.

- Principal appreciated my efforts and stopped by to let me know with examples.
- Our nine-week student recognition ceremonies--recognizing students' achievements.
- A time during a team meeting where I felt valued and helpful sharing skills/interventions with other teachers.
- Colleague time, during recess time—the teachers who I don't see much since they teach in other grade levels or parts of the building.... became my friends both personally and professionally.
- Getting a note from a former student who I had here at the elementary school when she came by to visit and stated that I am the reason she went into teaching.
- The staff party, realizing I liked the people I worked with, getting to meet their families and knowing them beyond the day to day; I felt accepted, comfortable.
- The principal. She guided me through the teacher evaluation process, so I could organize a portfolio for success with documentation; she cared and supported me.

(continued)

Background	Description	Sample Questions used to Guide the 4-D Cycle	Sample Responses
Step 1 in the AI 4-D Cycle: Discovery			
	Share stories (the best from the past) to discover strengths, values, and wishes.	What do you value most about this district? Your school? About teaching?	**What I value most about this district, my school, and about teaching:** • Working toward a goal with my teacher team, running in a 5K in support of a student with leukemia or creating a new themed unit with my team. • Seeing a child grow, mature, and succeed. • The relationship with other teachers. • Colleague trust and learning from others. • Spending time with the kids. • Having choices and allowed to be creative. • Sharing. • Being there for the kids and each other.
	Share stories (the best from the past) to discover strengths, values, and wishes.	What three wishes do you have for the district? Your school? Your team?	**Three wishes:** • More consistency in my grade level teacher teams rather than two new people every year. • Everyone trusts each other. • A more welcoming school. • Principals let the teachers help make decisions. • The school need to be inviting and more positive. • More time to meet.

			• Time to get to know the principal. • Someone who listens—maybe more social times we used to be a great school, but I do not even know half of the people as there are so many new people anymore.
1. Discovery (Roles)	Part B. Identify the themes and determine what's most valued, best practices, strengths.	• Review the data and highlight or color code repeated phrases or put in a spreadsheet. • List most common phrases on big chart paper; review the data for success factors discuss and vote on those most valued by the individuals. • Post votes (e.g., 3 dots to each person or use a conference live voting system with clicker/smartphones).	• Combination of what's most valued, strengths of the school/district, best practices. • Inviting school, positive climate. • Trust. • Build relationships. • Collaborative decision-making. • Appreciation/recognition.

Table 5.2 Teacher retention: the AI 4-D cycle dream phase

		Step 2 in the AI 4-D Cycle: Dream	
Step	**Description**	**Sample Questions Used to Guide the 4-D Cycle**	**Sample Responses**
2. Dream (Possible Plays)	Part A. Imagine future possibilities of what could be.	If the impossible were possible, what three wishes would you have so teachers would be lined up to work in the #1 rated district in the state.	**If the impossible were possible:** • Clarity in a common vision. • Staff were role models without agendas. • Promoted positive school climates, inviting to parents. • Acknowledge and address diversity. • District/school provided all the resources / technology necessary. • Our district is good, but what if it were great?!…The BEST!

		Three years have passed. What has attracted teachers? What are you seeing and what are they saying about the district?	• Pay scale was similar to other professionals like doctors, accountants, and lawyers.
			• Each *school* had a common vision.
			• Every school had a principal as leader who:
			  • had a positive, working relationship with all of his/her teachers.
			  • valued teachers professionally.
			  • allowed shared decision-making.
			  • could manage change.
			  • held people accountable.
			  • could effectively communicate.

			• was able to help teachers align beliefs with the district expectations (same philosophy about kids, teaching, learning, managing behaviors). • could provide appropriate teacher preparation and valuable staff development.
2. Dream (Possible Plays)	Part B. Identify the themes, and determine what's most valued, best practices, strengths.	• Review the data and highlight or color code repeated phrases or put in a spreadsheet. • List most common phrases on big chart paper; review the data for success factors discuss and vote on those most valued by the individuals. • Post votes (e.g., 3 dots to each person or use a conference live voting system with clicker/smartphones). • Options for clarification are to review results through wish or dream statements (e.g., create a video, act out a skit, draw a mural or metaphor, write a story/poem, song) before writing vision statements.	Some items were important, but others ranked higher. Intrinsic/extrinsic rewards with salary were more of an occupational prestige notion and had fewer dots thus less important than creating a positive school climate and projecting a good to great district image, addressing early career teacher needs/mentoring and those transitioning into education, and development of leadership especially for principals were higher priorities. Priorities: • Priority 1—most votes: Promote positive image for district (begin with elementary schools). • Priority 2—second most votes: Increase principal leadership capacity • Priority 4—Teacher collaboration—how to successfully implement PLCs so collective instructional decisions can be made including decisions about students. • Priority 3—third most votes: Work toward a positive school climate by fostering principal-teacher and teacher-teacher relationships. • Priority 5—Promote inclusiveness.

Table 5.3 Teacher retention: the AI 4-D cycle design phase

Step		Step 3 in the AI 4-D Cycle: Design	
	Description	Sample Questions used to Guide the 4-D Cycle	Sample Responses
3. Design (Game Plan)	Create bold statements (vision statements) of an idealized future merging the best of what is valued with the ideal future. Prioritize and gain consensus of what should be.	Take the best from 1B (Discovery) and 2B (Dream) steps to create the bold vision statements. Ask, does the design use all the most important factors from the lists created in the discovery and dream phases? In pairs, begin to create the bold statements and share out to larger groups until consensus is reached addressing the four priority Ps: • people (who we are and who are we when we are at our best); • purpose (our goal), • principles (what we value and believe), and • practices (the world we want to live in and create together as a teacher team).	Brainstorming of ideas: People: teachers—passionate—leaders, leading by example Purpose: help students grow academically, socially, emotionally, behaviorally; project positive image. Principles: trust, able to take risks, open/flexible, advocate for all students. Promote inclusiveness. Practices: want excellence; lifelong learners, want a positive learning environment.

	Our vision for the workplace:	**Our vision for the workplace as elementary teachers: who we are and at our best:** All teachers project their passion for excellence in teaching and learning at all times, leading by example.
	Our purpose:	**Our purpose:** We help project a positive image of the district knowing our contagious energy is invigorating. We strive for an environment that cultivates academic growth and social and emotional development in all children that surpasses all expectations, preparing students for success.
	Our commitment to job satisfaction, teacher retention efforts, and to each other:	**Our commitment to job satisfaction and to each other:** We thrive in an environment that genuinely cares for each other that is safe and supportive on and off the field (in or out of school). We share, laugh, cry, risk, grow, and learn from each other. We are family.

developed, yet written in present tense. The process and sample responses are provided.

Table 5.4 is the fourth step in the AI 4-D cycle and is called the destiny phase. The discussions in the destiny phase are centered around determining what it will take to make the dream come true. Descriptions, sample guiding questions, and a sampling of responses are provided. Creating an action plan and committing to the action plan are detailed in Table 5.5.

Action plan

Table 5.5 is the action plan co-constructed by approximately 130 participants as a part of the fourth step in the AI 4-D cycle, the destiny phase. The action plan is focused on the participants' top priority, which was to promote a positive image of the district beginning with the elementary schools. The group decided the first task was to launch a positive image campaign. Table 5.5 shows the five steps taken to launch the campaign.

Summary: Chapter 5 playbook for Scenario 1—increasing teacher retention

Logistics

The Playbook for Scenario 1 example focused on teacher retention at the elementary level. The five elementary schools and their principals participated in the two-day event, plus three district level directors or assistant superintendents. Participants met in an elementary, multipurpose room that had a small stage area, wireless microphones, and large screen with a projector. A countdown timer was used to help groups stay on task and pace their discussions. Large chart paper, markers, tape, and pens were on each table. Participants sat at round tables with chairs. Participants could either sit with those they were familiar with from their schools or could be mixed where the majority are from other schools; the preference is that participants will sit where there are only 2–3 from the same school at each table, so they have an opportunity to meet new friends from the beginning.

The AI process is a highly participatory learning journey, so the final decision was left up to the facilitator, who requested that no more than 2–3 people per school sit at the same table. Scenario 1 example was designed to be held over a two-day period, known as an AI event or summit. The AI summit

Table 5.4 Teacher retention: the AI 4-D cycle destiny phase

	Step 4 in the AI 4-D Cycle: Destiny		
Step	**Description**	**Sample Questions used to Guide the 4-D Cycle**	**Sample Responses**
4. Destiny (Playbook)	Create and commit to the action plan and to sustaining the plan, making it happen!	What will it take to make the dream come true? Create an action plan, a detailed plan outlining the steps to accomplish the goal(s) with an implementation timeline: address processes, people, resources that need to be in place, timelines, and celebration milestones. The action plan should answer the 4Ws + 2Hs: Who, What, Where, When, plus How and How much. • Write goals/SMART goals, decide on deadlines. • List the activities or tasks that need to be completed. • Create the action plan so progress can be monitored and reviewed, reprioritized, etc. • Commit to the task or action you complete ((List three ways you can help contribute to achieving the plan).	Action plans were written for the top three priorities. This example shows the action plan for Priority 1 in Table 5.5. Priority 1: Promote positive image for district (begin with elementary schools) *See the Action Plan, Table 5.5 for the SMART goal and tasks to launch a positive image campaign for the district, focused on the elementary schools.* Priority 2: Increase principal leadership capacity (Chapter 6). Priority 3: Work toward a positive school climate by fostering principal-teacher and teacher-teacher relationships.

Table 5.5 Teacher retention: the AI 4-D cycle destiny phase calls for action planning with commitment

	Sample Action Plan—Destiny Phase Elementary Teacher Retention
Overall Objective: In two years, the district's elementary schools will have an average retention rate of 90% (excludes retirees) an 18.5% increase.	
Current Situation: The current average retention rate for the five elementary schools over the past five years (excluding retirees) is at 73% with the past year's average at 71%.	
Priority 1: Promote a positive image for the district--Year 1 focus on elementary schools: Goal 1: District leadership and elementary level educators will intentionally promote a positive image for the district at any opportunity given within the district or outside the district when communicating with others over the next year.	
Task 1: Launch positive image campaign	

What Action Step Description	Who Person/Dept. Responsible	When Begin Date	When Due Date	How Materials/ Resources Needed	How Much	Notes
Step 1: Critique/upgrade district website and school web links to "amazing" level to include district/school facts and weekly school pictures of activities highlighting achievements, community involvement. Repeat same message to all other social media venues—Facebook,	Webmaster; Communications (APC) Director, website designer	Jan 13	Mar 8	Hire website designer expert over 1 year—consultant—approx 80-90 hours	$6,760	Multiple meetings and discussions between tech/ webmaster and APC communications departments and expert website designer
	School principals; site councils, webmaster, APC Director; school tech teams	Week of Feb 16	Feb 16, 17, 19, 23	Partner with school councils for input/critiquing changes—meetings Feb 16, 17, 19, 23		Critique & analysis with school councils—completed

Activity	Person Responsible				Notes
Twitter, Instagram, Wikipedia, LinkedIn, local TV station, etc.	Webmaster; Communications (APC) Director	Feb 17	Mar 8	In Kind	Continue to make adjustments based on feedback
Step 2: Reorganize focus for district communication office to include strategic advocacy, partnerships, & communications (APC) linking school-community	Superintendent & APC director; all involved in past year; Food Service	Jan 20, 2021	Jan 3, 2022	Soup and salad luncheon for employees	Celebrate district/school accomplishments at Inservice
a. District communication staff assigned to specific buildings	APC director with communication staff	Jan 23	Jan 23		Micki to CES Aaron to FES Jackie to VES DeVonte to MES
b. Brand our image-values, quality schools, accomplishments	APC staff; Principals, All staff/employees	Jan 23	Ongoing		Plans presented to all elementary employees at May staff development day

(continued)

Task 1: Launch positive image campaign

What Action Step Description	Who Person/Dept. Responsible	When Begin Date	When Due Date	How Materials/ Resources Needed	How Much	Notes
c. Sharing Our Story: build credibility through storytelling: parents, teachers, students, alumni	APC director & staff;	Jan 23	Ongoing	Ideas submitted to APC Director at District Office		First story aired March 7-small local business owner shares what the district has meant to their family with four generations attending district – four generations featured in video
d. Perception – Education Foundation with Billboards.com for school advertising	APC Director; Education Foundation Director, HR Director & Superintendent, ClearChannel	Mar 25	Dec 30	Advertising funded by District Education Foundation Endowment	$18,000	"71% of drivers consciously look at billboards while driving" (https://harleysdream.org/2019/02/07/billboard-advertising-statistics/). Two billboards × 5 months-Aug-Dec $1,800 × 2 × 5 months

e. Perception – Host Realtor's Luncheon with school tours, and	School Superintendent, Board members, APC director & staff; local realty assoc.; Food service director	Sept 1	Oct 19	Meet with Food service -Sept 3 for both	One elementary school (FES) was host; 5th grade students led tours
				Send out invitations-Sept 12 & Oct 1; follow up Oct 15;	
				Thank you's to be sent Oct 20—APC staff	
f. Perception – Host state legislative members breakfast & tour	School Superintendent, Board members, APC director & staff; contact legislative members; Food service director	Sept 1	Nov 9	Meet with Food service -Sept 3 for both events	One elementary school (VES) was host; 5th grade students led tours
				Send out invitations-Sept 12 & Oct 1; follow up Nov 2;	
				Thank you's to be sent Nov 10-APC staff	

(continued)

Task 1: Launch positive image campaign

What Action Step Description	Who Person/Dept. Responsible	When Begin Date	When Due Date	How Materials/ Resources Needed	How Much	Notes
g. Host Charity 5K (student JJ with cancer) during Fall Festival/River Festival	APC Director, Community Fall Festival director, Mayor who works with city fire/police, HS athletic director, director of school nurses, principals, Family of JJ-elem. student w/cancer; HS KAYs sponsor & group	July 23	Oct 14	Planning meetings throughout this time with APC Director & Fall Festival Director, then established details from there—Aug 3, Aug 15, etc. KAYs in charge of volunteers from community & schools—also all thank you notes to sponsors, businesses, volunteers Athletic Director & Mayor—5K route; Football coaches/ team water stations with the school nurses		KAYs is a high school coed service, character-building, & leadership club.

				Sponsors-APC Director & Fall Festival Director	
h. Host free community - family "Movie Night" on the football field	APC Director, HS athletic director, principals, superintendent, tech director and as needed staff	Aug 2	Sept 10	APC communicates via social media avenues and flyers home for each school; principals contacted partnerships for food sponsorships and give aways.	VES had 34% of students in attendance at game Sept 17. CES -27% MES-55% FES-49% Snacks provided by Walmart and others
i. Highlight one elementary school before the HS football game each Friday night (students & their families from that school get in free)	APC Director, HS athletic director, principals, superintendent, tech with three min video of featured school	Aug 2	VES video by Sept 10 School Recognition Dates: VES: Sept 17 CES: Sept 24	APC communicates via social media avenues and flyers home for each school	VES had 34% of students in attendance at game Sept 17. Others: CES -27% MES-55% FES-49%

(continued)

Task 1: Launch positive image campaign

What Action Step Description	Who Person/Dept. Responsible	When Begin Date	When Due Date	How Materials/Resources Needed	How Much	Notes
			MES: Oct 8			PTO: Sponsored Pizza Party to MES for the highest number of attendees.
			FES: Oct 16			
Step 3: Each school reviews, updates, & promotes clear vision, mission statements, mascot, school slogan/ tagline, and produces three-five positive facts about school/district for school website: Begin to Share Our Story	Teacher teams, principals.	May 4 (teacher staff development day-building level)	June 10	School Presentations at School Council Meeting with feedback, revised.		Example District Facts: Rated as an "A" school district four consecutive years!
		May 16-June 3		Final presentations at Superintendent's meeting		Growing district for the past 12 years serving 6,300+ students
						Growing graduation rate of 92.4%

Step 4: Each school submits at least two weekly highlights to the communications office (APC).	Elem. principals, APC liaison to each school, lead teacher for each teacher team	Jan 22	Ongoing-weekly	Posted on school websites and some on the district website	Each school submitted pictures/short 30 second videos highlighting events. EX:
					5th: Science projects with new PLTW program
					4th: Thank you cards for soldiers, local police & fire
					3rd: Time with Seniors—Valentine Cards to the VA Hospital
					2nd: Collection hub for newspapers, old towels for Humane Center for dogs & cats
					1st: Acts of Kindness: Collect donations for Kindness Baskets for elderly in community

(continued)

Task 1: Launch positive image campaign

What Action Step Description	Who Person/Dept. Responsible	When Begin Date	When Due Date	How Materials/ Resources Needed	How Much	Notes
Step 5: Connect Human Resources (HR) & Employees	HR dept.	Jan 13	Ongoing			
a. Build internal employee promoters to help showcase district/school	HR director, principals	Jan 26	Ongoing	Initial list of high performing teachers— energetic, enthusiastic		
b. Share district/school story	HR director, APC director, principals	June 8	Aug 21	Coordinate school featured videos with fall football games: VES: Sept 17 CES: Sept 24 MES: Oct 8 FES: Oct 16		Videos for each school completed by Sept 3. Videos shown and well received before each football game.Completed on schedule with recognition of students/families from each school.

c. Focus on collaborative work culture—clarity of vision, energy, enthusiasm, high performing employees—highlight with short videos	HR director, principals, APC dept.	Mar 23	Ongoing	Recognized at Board meetings and at Teacher Development Days; post to websites/social media	
d. Highlight employee Heroes: Employee of the month or Attitude of the month, Teacher of the Year	HR director, principals, APC dept.	Aug 4 (start w/Back to School)	Ongoing	Recognized at Board meetings and at Teacher Development Days; post to websites/social media; local TV	
e. Host teacher hiring fairs and offer a day of job shadowing in the district	HR director, principals, APC dept., teachers	Fall: Oct 9 and Spring Jan 20, 2022	Fair dates: Dec 3, 2021 / April 8	Notify Board of Regents' colleges; area private colleges	
f. Host vaccine clinic	HR director, principals, APC dept., County Health dept., school nurses, food service	Jan 1	Mar 23 & April 26	Notify all district employees & community—Mar 12;	Completed.

(continued)

Task 1: Launch positive image campaign

What Action Step Description	Who Person/Dept. Responsible	When Begin Date	When Due Date	How Materials/ Resources Needed	How Much	Notes
				APC videos and interviews on location along with TV media; post to social media		800 doses available— Moderna (Two vaccines; two dates) All slots filled. News 6 on site.
Action Plan Review Dates Destiny (Playbook)	Those who participated in the AI process, creating & implementing the action plan	May 12		Host: FES Library		Checkpoint
		July 25		Host: MES Multipurpose Rm		Checkpoint
		Sept 10		Host: CES Library		Checkpoint
		Dec 10		Host: District Conf Rm		Plan Jan 3 district-wide in-service celebration with soup/salad luncheon

began with a welcome by the superintendent and facilitator; the superintendent stated the purpose for the event and encouraged participation by all attending. The facilitator reviewed the agenda providing an overview for Day 1, asked that participants introduce themselves at their table group, and share a favorite app on their phone. A sample two-day agenda can be found in Chapter 9. The process of establishing team norms or ground rules was next and becomes a practice run, so participants understand the process and expectations when engaged in the AI 4-D cycle. This step is truly valuable when maintaining a sense of orderliness and acknowledging that everyone's time is valued. The process for establishing team norms or ground rules was discussed in Chapter 4.

The 4-Ds

The discovery phase asked people to work in pairs and answer four initial questions: a past, personal story; high point, outstanding experiences; characteristics in others they value or what they value; and wishes for the future. Refer to Table 5.1. In the Scenario 1 example, each pair shared what most attracted them to the district. They described a high point experience when they were most proud to be an employee, what they valued most about the district, school, or being a teacher, and three wishes for their district or school. The pairs were asked to share each other's stories and experiences at their assigned small table groups of 8–10 people. Common themes were determined and shared with other small table groups until final sets of lists had been created and posted for viewing by the whole group. Each person was given a set of three sticky dots to place by the phrases which they personally valued most. The whole group could then view which items were valued most by everyone in the room. Having a process to help identify themes and determining what the group values, what they feel are best practices or what's working to retain teachers and their building's strengths and consideration for the district's strengths help the large group with decision making. In this case, participants were asked to review the shared data at their table groups of 8–10 people and highlight or color code repeated phrases or put in a spreadsheet. They listed the most common phrases on big chart paper; reviewed the data for success factors discussed and voted on those most valued by the individuals in their table groups. Two table groups are combined who share their work and then combine their lists. The process is repeated until there are only two groups remaining.

All participants form one group and post votes (e.g., three dots to each person or use a conference live voting system where the lists are posted on a screen/interactive board and live voting with clicker/smartphones occurs then group results can be displayed (e.g., Poll Everywhere, n.d.). Options to review results through visual images can include charts, pictures, metaphors, puzzles, concept maps to gain further clarifications on meaning and intent. The grouping process was described in Chapter 3, much like the single elimination brackets using 16 numbered tables in Chapter 3, Figure 3.6.

The dream phase (Table 5.2) asked participants to take the best from the past or current situation and wishes from the discovery phase and imagine future possibilities for attracting staff to their school or district. The dream phase asked participants to dream big, if the impossible were possible. Participants were asked to imagine that time had elapsed, and the dream had become reality. They were asked to describe what was happening around them, addressing what people were saying or seeing. Participants in groups, either one or two table groups (8–20) were asked to create a video, act out a skit, draw a mural or create a metaphor, write a story/poem, song to help with the vision. The creations, which were skits and songs/raps, were shared with the whole group.

The third step in the AI 4-D cycle, the design phase, asked participants to create bold, vision statements defining who they were and where they wanted to be, based on the imagined future in the dream phase. The design phase bridges the discovery and dream phases, so bold, vision statements can be co-constructed based on what is valued and what the wishes or dreams are for the school and district. Participants went through the process of prioritizing their dream statements and visualized or acted out the statements so they were better able to determine what should be. Found in Table 5.3, they wrote bold, vision (provocative propositions) statements that included a vision, a purpose, and a commitment after considering the four priority Ps: people (who we are and who are we when we are at our best); purpose (our goal), principles (what we value and believe), and practices (the world we want to live in and create together). How to make the bold, vision statements come true then becomes the final, destiny phase.

The destiny phase is the action and commitment to realizing the future. Table groups were asked to detail what it would take to make the vision statements come true in the form of action plans, working on Priority 1 from the design phase. Priority 1, as noted in Table 5.4 was to promote a positive image for the district. Together the groups developed goals, tasks, and action steps that would need to occur to make Priority 1 a reality. The co-constructed action plan, Table 5.5, stated Task 1 as launching a positive image campaign that included five major steps. Each table group created their lists and then shared with other table groups. Once the information was paired down to four groups, the groups shared out to the whole group and then placed their listed ideas on a timeline posted along one of the walls made from bulletin board paper, as to the order of what made sense in terms of what should happen first, then second. The timeline example can be found in Chapter 9, Table 9.3.

Once there was consensus over the action plan steps for Task 1 in launching the positive image campaign for the district primarily for the elementary schools in Year 1, the details were completed and participants were asked how they would personally contribute to making the dream happen? The process was then repeated for Priorities 2 and 3 with action plans completed. Participants were encouraged to make a personal commitment to at least one of the three priorities (forming action groups). The facilitator addressed how the priority action groups would be contacted after the AI event to sustain the momentum and keep the action alive. The two-day AI summit closed with participants completing an "Exit Ticket" and having an opportunity to share (open microphone) comments and reflections.

Sustaining the plan

The momentum and sustaining the action plan continued with the creation and work from action groups. The action plan timeline was from January through December with three checkpoint dates bringing everyone together; one occurred via an online Zoom session. The Year 1 celebration had been included in the action plan (Table 5.5) scheduled for January, and the celebration planning became one of the action groups. Action groups, those who committed to work on the various steps, were comprised of the AI 4-D participants committed to making the plan happen. They explained their purpose in fulfilling the action plan goals to other building staff, parents, alumni, business, and community members who later joined and helped the action groups achieve the goals as the year progressed. An action group was formed called *social media reviewers* with the goal of critiquing and helping to create a website with the hired expert web designer. They also helped promote several other social media sites such as setting up school Twitter and Instagram accounts. There was a school to district-district to school action group that helped with communication and submissions of school events, creating the school highlight videos and promoting the recognition of each school during the fall football games. There was an action group that created a "Teacher Feature" recognizing the outstanding work of teachers.

The energy and possibilities were felt throughout the district with multiple inquiries if something were a possibility such as, a "Hall of Famers" that was established through the educational foundation to recognize outstanding alumni and retired educators. Rather than administrators attending employment fairs, a teacher employment fair was established on site and is held annually where pre-service teachers, new graduates, and experienced teachers are encouraged to join the district for a full day of events to tour the district, have lunch, and go through the interview process. Guests at the employment fair were encouraged to spend an additional day in the district paired with a teacher to observe and shadow so the potential hire could get a glimpse at district, building, and teacher expectations.

Priority 1 was expanded to encompass staff in grades 7–12 where the AI change model was used to envision possibilities for teacher retention at the secondary levels which occurred in Year 2. The hiring and retention of special education teachers was addressed during that process as well. The AI 4-D cycle being a solutions-based, decision-making process, helped establish a process where teachers who were interested in becoming special education teachers could join a district cohort group and work toward a master's degree in special education at one of the state Board of Regents' universities; it was agreed that a portion of tuition would be covered by the district. A teacher rotation process was also discussed regarding teachers moving into a special education position for two years and then back into a general education classroom for 2–5 years and then back into special education for another two years.

Elementary teachers voiced their wishes during the discovery and dream phases of the AI 4-D cycle and became Priorities 2 and 3 in the destiny phase. Action plans for Priorities 2 and 3 were then addressed by the district's administrative team.

Priority 2 (Table 5.2) was focused on increasing principal leadership capacity where the task responsibilities fell more at the district level and were addressed administratively with the district leadership team (see Chapter 6). The data and information gathered from the AI 4-D cycle were used as the assistant superintendent and superintendent worked with the principals individually and in administrative meetings to help develop leadership skills. The meetings were designed specifically to address the information gleaned from the AI 4-D cycle, found in Table 5.2.

Priority 3 (Table 5.2) was working toward a more positive school climate by fostering principal-teacher and teacher-teacher relationships. The building administrator(s) addressed Priority 3 action plan tasks and monitored progress focused on a district-wide topic. They started by creating a shared vision, determining core beliefs, and school-wide behaviors for students, staff, and families. The elementary schools held their own one-day AI summit and included parents and previously established business and community partnerships in the process as they addressed school climate. They created an action plan specific to their building using the AI 4-D cycle, making positive changes toward the school's climate and culture (see Chapter 6).

This chapter has provided a *how-to* playbook with step-by-step details using the AI 4-D cycle with the discovery, dream, design, and destiny phases centered around the topic of a district-wide issue, teacher retention. Approximately 130 administrative staff and building teachers participated in the two-day event. The action plan for Priority 1 was included. A summary of the two-day AI summit with logistics and brief notes on the 4Ds was shared. A sample two-day agenda can be found in Chapter 9.

The momentum from conversations and the energy of participants grew throughout the two days and was at an all-time high when co-creating the action plan with innovative steps to improve the district's image. The participants were asked to commit to making their wishes or dream become a reality by serving on one of the many action groups. Throughout the year the excitement continued and grew as others joined the efforts from the secondary schools and community. Chapter 6, Playbook for Scenario 2—Building a Strong Leadership Team stems from Priority 2 (Table 5.2) addressing how to increase principal leadership capacity.

Reference

Poll Everywhere. (n.d.). Instant poll voting on smartphones. Retrieved August 13, 2022, from https://www.polleverywhere.com/smartphone-web-voting

6

Playbook for Scenario 2—building a strong leadership team

Topic or focus of inquiry—how does my leadership behavior support staff and influence student learning?

This chapter, the playbook for Scenario 2, focuses on the topic of developing leadership skills and behaviors and asks the question, *how does my leadership behavior support staff and influence student learning?* The voices of elementary teachers in Chapter 5 helped the district administration realize there was a crucial need to help the district's administrative team develop the leadership skills necessary to lead their buildings.

The elementary staff were given the opportunity to imagine what the district could be if the impossible was possible to address teacher retention in Chapter 5. One of the solutions and the top priority was promoting a positive image for the district, beginning with the elementary schools. The second priority, which is the focus of this chapter, was to increase principal leadership capacity. Teachers defined the phrase, "increasing principal leadership capacity" to mean: Every school had a principal who was a leader, who could develop a positive, working and trusting relationship with all staff, yet hold people accountable. The definition also included a principal who could effectively communicate, manage change, and was able to help teachers align their beliefs with the district expectations (e.g., same philosophy about kids, teaching, learning, managing behaviors). The teachers also felt building leadership meant, the principal, as leader, should help create a positive school environment where teachers felt valued professionally, were allowed to be

DOI: 10.4324/9781003350804-6

part of the decision-making process, and where teacher preparation was considered valuable in helping staff grow professionally.

This chapter focuses on leadership development among the district's administrators and describes the appreciative inquiry (AI) 4-D cycle in Table 6.1 with sample questions used to guide the discussions along with selected responses made by building administrators. The four steps in the AI 4-D cycle are reviewed first with the co-created action plan. A summary of the chapter and sustaining the dream with follow up information are included. Agendas are found in Chapter 9.

Those participating in the Scenario 2 example were PreK-12 building level administrators, the school district superintendent, the district's special education coordinator, and the assistant superintendent as facilitator. The AI 4-D cycle was held for one day in the summer and then continued throughout the school year with regularly scheduled two-hour meetings two times per month. The meetings took place in the district's conference center in a large room that had access to a partial kitchen. Four round tables with seating for eight people at each table were in the center of the room. Additional rectangle tables were around the perimeter of the room for activities where people were paired or worked in groups with four people.

Tables 6.1–6.4 detail the AI 4-D cycle: Discovery, Dream, Design, and Destiny. Included are the guiding questions and a selection of responses. Table 6.5 shows the action plan that includes the objective and priorities as established in the 4-D process, goals, tasks, timelines, and responsible parties. The action plan became the opportunity to enhance leadership development through participation in the activities and resulted in behavior changes.

The AI 4-D cycle

Table 6.1 lists the four types of questions used in the AI 4-D cycle discovery phase: Sharing past stories of a leader they admire or the qualities of an extraordinary leader. Referencing their own leadership experiences, administrators were asked to list qualities or skills that mattered most in a leader; what they valued most about being a school or district administrator, and three wishes for their leadership team. Next, they identified the themes, then voted on the three that matter most. Several responses are provided from participants.

Table 6.2 shows the questions used in the second step of the AI 4-D cycle, known as the dream phase. The first part asks participants to imagine future possibilities of what could be—related to leadership capacity focused on how

Table 6.1 Leadership development with the district administrative team: the AI 4-D cycle discovery phase

Background	Description	Sample Questions Used to Guide the 4-D Cycle	Sample Responses
Topic	Area of focus for change, innovation:	How does my leadership behavior support staff and influence student learning?	
Participants	Who needs to be involved in the change process?	• 26 administrators.	• 8 building principals, 9 assistant principals, 1 special education coordinator, 1 athletic director, 1 superintendent, 2 assistant superintendents—director of elementary and director of secondary services, 1 curriculum director, 1 preschool coordinator, 1 district assessment coordinator, and 1 facilitator (another assistant superintendent). Total: 25 participants; 1 facilitator

Step 1 in the AI 4-D Cycle: Discovery

Step	Description	Sample Questions Used to Guide the 4-D Cycle	Sample Responses
1. Discovery (Roles)	Part A. Share stories (the best from the past) to discover strengths, values, and wishes.	Describe a person you admire or consider to be an extraordinary leader. What qualities do they possess that are effective, really matter, or make a difference?	**Leadership qualities:** • Communicates well. • Builds relationships/friendly. • Trustworthy/dependable/consistent/credible. • Good with people/positive/enthusiastic. • He leads by example/they walk the talk. • Listens. • Very respectful. • Supports others' ideas/promotes others. • Knowledgeable/competent. • Not afraid/innovator/change agent/maverick. • Values others opinions/seeks advice/shares in the decision-making/values collaboration.
		Describe a high point experience where you were most proud to be a building/school administrator. Who was involved? What was happening?	**High Point Experience as a school administrator:** • When the high school was recognized as a Blue Ribbon school and the students were cheering; I felt appreciated and supported. • When I was asked to co-chair the all-day kindergarten initiative, and our efforts and time were well worth it when the Board accepted the proposal. • Helping students learn how to help others with the food drive for a local charity or the Thanksgiving dinner where our students served the community lunch. • Participating in the district golf fundraiser.

(continued)

Background	Description	Sample Questions Used to Guide the 4-D Cycle	Sample Responses
			• When I was a part of a secondary team that worked with district office to complete applications and got the Career and Technical Education pathways Law, Security & Public Safety and the Hospitality & Tourism accepted by the state. • Having graduation celebrations as the alternative high school students complete graduation credits throughout the year. • When one of our special education students asked me to be his fishing partner on his end of school year fieldtrip. • Speaking at graduation.
	Share stories (the best from the past) to discover strengths, values, and wishes.	Based on your leadership experiences, what skills or qualities matter most?	**High Point Experience at Building Level:** • Helping others be successful/being there for the kids. • Leading by example. • Colleague time with my building administrative team—sharing experiences. • Being effective by communicating the same message over and over…the story about your attitude. • Communicates the truth and respects others equally. • Communicating with consistency in relation to teacher expectations. • Being visible.

| Share stories (the best from the past) to discover strengths, values, and wishes. | What do you value most about being a school or district administrator? | **What I value most about this district, my school, and about teaching:**

• Seeing students succeed/helping students.
• Forming relationships with others: Teachers, students, parents.
• Trust. |
| Share stories (the best from the past) to discover strengths, values, and wishes. | What three wishes do you have for the district? Your school? Your leadership team? | **Three wishes:**

• Have something for our students who meet our expectations especially behaviors.
• Teacher collaboration, more teacher cohesion within their teams.
• Teachers analyzing student data and responding.
• Patience and trust for others.
• Knowing what the research says—discipline/PBIS.
• Figure out MTSS (RtI).
• A shared sense of "us"/common vision.
• PBIS implementation help/how to help improve student behaviors, motivation.
• Additional staff.
• How to help the teacher departments/PLCs that can't get along/how to help teacher teams accomplish what needs to get done. |

(continued)

Background	Description	Sample Questions Used to Guide the 4-D Cycle	Sample Responses
1. Discovery (Roles)	Part B. Identify the themes and determine what is most valued, best practices, strengths.	• Review the data and highlight or color code repeated phrases or put in a spreadsheet. • List most common phrases on big chart paper; review the data for success factors discuss and vote on those most valued by the individuals. • Post votes (e.g., 3 dots to each person or use a conference live voting system with clicker/ smartphones).	Combination of what's most valued, strengths of the school/ district, best practices… • Lead by doing/modeling behavior. • Trust. • Build relationships. • Collaborative decision-making. • Appreciation/recognition. • Common vision; communicate and focus on the vision. • Professional development on what the research and implementation practices: PBIS, MTSS, social, emotional, and academic growth.

Table 6.2 Leadership development with the district administrative team: step 2, the dream phase

Step	Description	Sample Questions Used to Guide the 4-D Cycle	Sample Responses
		Step 2 in the AI 4-D Cycle: Dream	
2. Dream (Possible Plays)	Part A. Imagine future possibilities of what could be.	To better support you, your students, and staff build a more positive, equitable, and supportive environment for student learning what three wishes would you act upon in this upcoming school year, if anything were possible?	**If the impossible were possible:** • Meaningful staff development that focused on the needs of our building. • Teacher collaboration time with an effective process—they need to get along and be productive, use data to help with decision-making. • Staff could learn to be role models without agendas; be professional. • How to work with disruptive teachers and students. • Reduce staff stress. • Have a place for disruptive students; behavior support and options available.

(continued)

Step	Description	Sample Questions Used to Guide the 4-D Cycle	Sample Responses
		Your wishes have come true throughout the year. As you wrap up the year describe what happened as you share stories with other building/ district administrators at the United School Administrators (USA) conference. Describe how your behaviors have changed to support staff and influenced student learning.	**Wishes have come true; the actions and behaviors of the teachers and administrators are united:** • Teachers-to-teachers and principals-teachers have positive, working relationships with each other. • Shared decision-making. • Consistency in student behaviors and behavior management systems—have the research and knowledge, one that works. • Teacher cohesion within departments/teacher teams and use data-driven decisions. • Everyone understands the goal/vision and are aligned with the district expectations (especially managing behaviors). • Time management: Developed a personal account (get to know each teacher) with each teacher and help them set goals. • More visible, greeting teachers in the morning, more walking around the building. • Communicating the vision & consistent expectations. • Staff development needs have been met.

2. **Dream** **(Possible Plays)**	Part B. Identify the themes, and determine what is most valued, best practices, strengths.	• Review the data and highlight or color code repeated phrases or put in a spreadsheet. • List most common phrases on big chart paper; review the data for success factors discuss and vote on those most valued by the individuals. • Post votes (e.g., 3 dots to each person or use a conference live voting system with clicker/smartphones). • Options for clarification are to review results through wish or dream statements (e.g., create a video, act out a skit, draw a mural or metaphor, write a story/poem, song) before writing vision statements.	Development of leadership especially for principals were higher priorities. Priorities: • Priority 1—most votes: Consistent student behavior management and responses to behavior that are research-based. • Priority 2—Teacher collaboration—bring more cohesion among teachers in departments/teacher teams/PLCs so collective instructional decisions can be made including decisions about students based on data. • Priority 3—Meet the needs of teachers in our buildings by providing meaningful staff development. • Priority 4—Positive and inviting school environment fostering principal-teacher and teacher-teacher relationships.

the administrators could help improve their school. They were asked to list three wishes for staff and students, and the last question asked them to project their wishes into the future as if their wishes had come true by the end of the school year. Sample responses are given. The second part of the dream phase had participants reviewing the data so themes could be identified.

Table 6.3 guides the district administrators through the design phase. The results from the first two phases, discovery and dream, are used to create the design phase where bold, vision statements of the future are developed, yet written in present tense.

Table 6.4 describes the fourth step, the destiny phase, in the AI 4-D cycle. The discussions in the destiny phase were centered around determining what it will take to make the dream come true. As part of the destiny phase, an action plan and commitment to the plan are detailed in Table 6.5.

Action plan

Table 6.5 is the action plan co-constructed by the 26 administrators as a part of the fourth step in the AI 4-D cycle, the destiny phase. The focus was on Priority 1, developing a plan to address student behavior management, discipline, and responses to behavior as determined in the AI 4-D cycle.

Summary: Chapter 6 playbook for Scenario 2—building a strong leadership team

Logistics

The Playbook for Scenario 2 example focused on leadership development in the form of helping the district administrative team work collaboratively toward solutions on a common issue or topic of focus: Consistent student behavior management and responses to behavior that are research-based. The district's administrative team participated in a one-day event. Participants met in one of the classrooms at the district's conference center. They brought their laptops and had large chart paper, markers, tape, and pens available on each of the four round tables.

The facilitator provided an overview for the day, had participants complete the introductions activity, then helped the group establish team norms or ground rules. The process for establishing team norms was a practice run, so participants understood the grouping process and expectations that carried

Table 6.3 Leadership development with the district administrative team: step three in the AI 4-D cycle, the design phase

Step		Description	Sample Questions Used to Guide the 4-D Cycle	Sample Responses
			Step 3 in the AI 4-D Cycle: Design	
3. Design (Game Plan)		Create bold statements (vision statements) of an idealized future merging the best of what is valued with the ideal future. Prioritize and gain consensus of what should be.	Take the best from 1B (Discovery) and 2B (Dream) steps to create the bold statements. Ask, does the design use all the most important factors from the lists created in the discovery and dream phases? In pairs, begin to create the bold statements and share out to larger groups until consensus is reached addressing the four priority Ps: • people (who we are and who are we when we are at our best), • purpose (our goal), • principles (what we value and believe), and • practices (the world we want to live in and create together as a teacher team).	Brainstorming of ideas: **People:** compassionate leaders, leading by example. **Purpose:** promote social, emotional, and academic growth of all students; provide materials/resources and professional development to improve instruction. **Principles:** trustworthy, positive, an advocate for all students, consistency in decision-making, collaborative. **Practices:** work with teachers to be effective in teacher teams/PLCs and in the classroom; promote and reward success, effectively; communicate goals, creation of positive learning environment, help others succeed.

(continued)

Step 3 in the AI 4-D Cycle: Design

Step	Description	Sample Questions Used to Guide the 4-D Cycle	Sample Responses
		Our vision for the workplace:	**Our vision as administrators: who we are and at our best:** We lead by being a visible example to all.
		Our purpose:	**Our purpose:** We are mediators of change. We provide consensus building processes to ensure our schools are supportive of the needs for staff and students.
		Our commitment to leadership behavior, and to each other:	**Our commitment:** We commit to more effective processes in developing prevention frameworks that promote social, emotional, and academic student growth.

Table 6.4 Leadership development with the district administrative team: step four in the AI 4-D cycle, the destiny phase

		Step 4 in the AI 4-D Cycle: Destiny	
Step	**Description**	**Sample Questions used to Guide the 4-D Cycle**	**Sample Responses**
4. Destiny (Playbook)	Create and commit to the action plan and to sustaining the plan, making it happen!	What will it take to make the dream come true? Create an action plan, a detailed plan outlining the steps to accomplish the goal(s) with an implementation timeline: address processes, people, resources that need to be in place, timelines, and celebration milestones. The action plan should answer the 4Ws + 2Hs: Who, What, Where, When, plus How and How much. • Write goals/SMART goals, decide on deadlines, • List the activities or tasks that need to be completed. • Create a visual so progress can be monitored and reviewed, reprioritized, etc. • Commit to the task or action you complete ((List three ways you can help contribute to achieving the plan).	The action plan for Priority 1 is detailed in Table 6.5. • Priority 1—most votes: Consistent student behavior management and responses to behavior that are research-based. • Priority 2—Teacher collaboration—bring more cohesion among teachers in departments/teacher teams/PLCs so collective instructional decisions can be made including decisions about students based on data (see Chapter 7). • Priority 3—Meet the needs of teachers in our buildings by providing meaningful staff development (see Chapter 8).

Table 6.5 Leadership development with the district administrative team: the AI 4-D cycle destiny phase calls for action planning with commitment

Action Plan—Destiny Phase Leadership Development
Overall Objective: Over the next school year, the district's administrative team will work collaboratively to implement a research-based positive behavior prevention framework for the elementary schools and one for the middle and high school with consistent terminology, definitions, and expectations.
Current Situation: Administrators report no consistency among schools, nor within their schools among staff regarding student discipline or responses to student behaviors. No defined teacher or principal roles when dealing with student behaviors. At the elementary, student discipline data may or may not be entered and reasons may be at the discretion of the person entering data. On a recent survey, 67% of K-12 building administrators rated their school's ability to help students develop social and emotional competencies between low to average. Only 40% of the building principals reported that 76% or more of their building's classrooms had a positive classroom environment (one where students feel welcome, safe, respected, and find learning to be supported along with their well-being).
Priority 1: Consistent student behavior management and responses to behavior that are research-based.
Goal 1: District leadership and building level administrators will intentionally work together, conducting research and determining a district-wide prevention framework on how to best address student behaviors and responses to behaviors with consistency among the preK-5 elementary schools and then establish a separate one for the middle school and high school.

Task 1: Collectively develop a plan to address student behavior management, discipline, and responses to behavior.

What Action Step Description	Who Person/Dept. Responsible	When Begin Date	When Due Date	How Materials/ Resources Needed	How Much	Notes
Step 1:						
Review available data: Data analysis of student discipline reported for past four years. • Analyze discipline reported in the student data management system. • Analyze screener data and student self-reporting data (e.g., SAEBRS, mySAEBRS)	Assistant Supt., District data tech, Administrative team: Building Principals	June 6, June 7	June 10	Laptops with excel, paper, pen.	Administrators on contract	Data analysis initial set of guiding questions developed by assistant superintendent: • Review how to use Excel data sort/pivot tables. • 3 hours both mornings: 8–11.

(continued)

Task 1: Collectively develop a plan to address student behavior management, discipline, and responses to behavior.

What Action Step Description	Who Person/Dept. Responsible	When Begin Date	When Due Date	How Materials/ Resources Needed	How Much	Notes
Step 2:						
Review how and where to conduct research to determine what works with student discipline. • Recommendations from state department. • Visit exemplary school modeling discipline prevention. • Review the literature-online databases. • Reach out to the professional organizations. • Review .gov websites	Assistant Supt., District data tech, Administrative team: Building Principals	June 8, June 9	July 12— report research	Laptops with excel, paper, pen.	Administrators on contract	3 hours both mornings: 8–11a.m. Example responses for possible review: PBIS/ MTSS /RtI. • Capturing Kids' Hearts. • Restorative Practices. • Social & Emotional Learning. • Bullying prevention. • Assertive Discipline. • Character Education. • AVID.

Activity	Responsible	Date		Materials		Notes
Share research findings on what works with student discipline	Assistant Supt., District data tech, Administrative team: Building Principals	July 12		Large chart paper, tape.		Three hours (8–11).
Step 3:						
Model the AI 4-D cycle with administrative team / principals practicing how to manage change and make decisions at the building level that involves staff in a collaborative, decision-making process: Topic of inquiry—addressing student behaviors & responses	Assistant Supt as AI facilitator, District data tech, Administrative team: Building Principals	July 13		Laptops with excel, paper, pen,	Administrators on contract	• To do list for step 4: • Review building discipline data—strengths questions. • Define discipline codes. • Create behavior matrix. • Classroom management training. • Define roles & expectations for teachers and for office referrals.
Prepare for step 4—principals pair up and co-facilitate the AI 4-D cycle simulating the July 12 event with their staff	Assistant Supt., District data tech, Administrative team: Building Principals	July 14	Aug 18			Copies of discipline data and codes.

(continued)

Task 1: Collectively develop a plan to address student behavior management, discipline, and responses to behavior.

What Action Step Description	Who Person/Dept. Responsible	When Begin Date	When Due Date	How Materials/Resources Needed	How Much	Notes
Step 4:						
Principals co-facilitate the AI 4-D cycle with teachers at the building level with principals leading the AI 4-D process practicing how to manage change with a collaborative process: • Topic of inquiry—addressing student behaviors & responses/ define classroom expectations and that for the office referrals	Building principals as co-facilitators; All licensed staff	Aug 18 am, then switch to the other principal's school Aug 18 p.m.	Aug 18			Address: • When, where, and how to teach social and emotional learning (SEL) skills. • Modeling. • School-wide student behavior incentive. • Individual student behavior incentives. • Build teacher-student relationships. • Motivation. • Monitoring/data portal. • Classroom environment.

Step 5:

Regularly planned administrative meetings to work toward leadership development	District Administrative team			3rd Thursday of each month- 9–11a.m. (Two hours).
Topics varied:				
Share Aug 18 process & action plans for addressing student behaviors	District Administrative team	Sept 16	• Process reactions. • Action plans.	
Report progress on action plans: student behaviors and a review of Aug 18 exit tickets & comments	District Administrative team	Oct 21	• Action plans. • Compiled summary of exit tickets from Aug 18 AI 4-D experience and accomplishments	Construed as positive at all levels.
Monitoring own leadership behaviors— influences on teachers and student learning	District Administrative team	Nov 18	Online survey and discussion.	• Promoting leadership capacity in staff. • Building relationships. • Collective purpose. • Supporting collaborative efforts.

(continued)

Task 1: Collectively develop a plan to address student behavior management, discipline, and responses to behavior.

What Action Step Description	Who Person/Dept. Responsible	When Begin Date	When Due Date	How Materials/ Resources Needed	How Much	Notes
Progress on action plans for topic of addressing student behaviors—results of Nov 11 staff development day.	District Administrative team	Dec 16		Results on staff development day, Nov 11 focused on action plans/ behaviors.		• Sensory room possibilities. • Results-visits to schools with sensory rooms.
Disciplinary decisions and changes in practices; social and emotional learning skills (SEL)	District Administrative team	Jan 19				• All elementaries aligned & in agreement. • 6–12 aligned & in agreement.

February In-service day—focus on positive classroom environment and review of teacher classroom rules/role of teacher in student discipline; de-escalation	District Administrative team	Jan 1 Feb 17	Feb 17	Results—to be discussed at March 16 meeting.	
Schoolwide behaviors, teacher and principal roles with behaviors	District Administrative team	March 16			
Action plan review	District Administrative team	April 20			
Celebration & prepare PBIS implementation fully for new school year	District Administrative team	June 7–8		Repeat processes for new school year.	Teacher communication & understanding imperative.

forward when engaged in the AI 4-D cycle. The process for establishing team norms or ground rules is found in Chapter 4.

The 4-Ds

The first step in the AI 4-D cycle was the discovery phase. The facilitator asked the administrators to work in pairs and answer four initial questions: a past, personal story; high point, outstanding experiences; characteristics in others they value or what they value; and wishes for the future. Table 6.1 shows questions used in the discovery phase. Each pair shared qualities and characteristics of an extraordinary leader they admired, described high point experiences when they were most proud to be a district or school administrator, what they valued most about being a school or district administrator, and based on their leadership experiences, what skills or qualities matter most. Lastly, they were asked to list three wishes for their school or district.

The pairs were asked to share each other's stories and experiences with their assigned small table group of 7–8 people. Themes were determined and shared with other table groups. Final priority lists were made through a vote by each person placing three sticky dots by the phrases most valued.

The dream phase (Table 6.2) was step two in the AI 4-D cycle. The school administrators were asked to take the best of the past or current situation and wishes from the discovery phase and imagine future possibilities, if the impossible were possible. They were also asked to fast forward to the end of the year, where the wishes and dreams have come true. They were asked to describe what happened to make their wishes and dreams come true as if they were sharing stories with other administrators at the United School Administrators (USA) June conference with a focus on how their behaviors as leaders had changed to support staff and influenced student learning. They reviewed their priorities and for clarification purposes, the groups, either individual tables (7–8 people) or as two combined table groups (14–16 people) were asked to create a video, act out a skit, draw a mural, create a metaphor, write a story/poem/song to help clarify the vision. The creations included a skit with a song/rap and a circus metaphor.

The design phase (Table 6.3), Step 3, takes the best from the discovery and dream phases and asked participants to create bold, vision statements. The bold, vision (provocative propositions) statements included the administrative team's vision, purpose, and commitment after considering the four priority Ps: People (who we are and who are we when we are at our best); purpose (our goal), principles (what we value and believe), and practices (the world we want to live in and create together).

The destiny phase, (Table 6.4) was the fourth step and focused on how to make the vision happen through action planning and commitment. The table groups focused on how to make Priority 1 come true: Consistent student behavior management and responses to behaviors that are research-based. Together the groups developed goals, tasks, and action steps that would need to occur to make Priority 1 a reality. The co-constructed action plan, Table 6.5, states Task 1 as collectively developing a plan to address student behavior management, discipline, and responses to behavior with five steps. Each table group brainstormed, created their 3–5 priority list, and then shared with the other table group. Once the information was paired down to two lists, the groups shared and then placed their listed ideas on a timeline (Chapter 9, Table 9.3) posted along one wall of the room in chronological order of what made sense in terms of what should happen and when.

Once there was consensus over the action plan steps for Task 1, the details were completed in the action plan template (Table 6.5) and participants were asked, how they would personally contribute to making the dream happen. In closing the day's event, the facilitator reminded administrators the next step was addressing Step 1 in the co-constructed action plan; she also reinforced what could be done immediately to sustain the momentum and keep the action alive. The administrators completed an "Exit Ticket" and had an opportunity to share before leaving.

Sustaining the plan

The district's administrative team began implementation of the action plan shortly after school ended for the year. Action plan (Table 6.5) Steps 1–3 were completed during the summer. They prepared for Step 4 and paired up with another administrator to implement Step 4 with their building staff during the August back-to-school in-service days. The background for this chapter was a result of Chapter 5.

If you recall, Chapter 5 used the AI 4-D cycle as a results-based model that brought about change, innovation, and solutions to increase teacher retention. Priority 1 was to create a positive image of the district. The second priority coming from the voice of approximately 120 teachers was the need to increase principal leadership capacity (Table 5.2).

The district level administrators began addressing leadership development in this chapter. They decided the best way to help building administrators develop their leadership skills was by providing opportunities to participate in a collaborative environment where learning, sharing, interacting, making collective decisions, and supporting each other was modeled.

This chapter provides the beginnings of a solution to leadership development or building leadership capacity with step-by-step details using the AI 4-D cycle using the Discovery, Dream, Design, and Destiny phases. The topic of focus or inquiry familiar to all K-12 building administrators was the development of consistent student behavior management and responses to behavior that were research-based. Addressing student discipline and behaviors as a district-wide focus of inquiry was used as the bridge to develop leadership among the principals.

The co-constructed action plan addressed the current discipline and student behavior's situation by learning how to review data already readily available to them (Table 6.5, Step 1). The principals had multiple conversations sharing experiences and learning more about the student discipline data. They also wanted to know how to conduct research and find evidence-based strategies with the goal of identifying positive behavior interventions and prevention frameworks that were working (Table 6.5, Step 2), which occurred on another morning. A partnership was formed with one of the local universities, so the administrative team had access to online databases. Another morning was used to share what they found from their research efforts.

Action plan Step 3 (Table 6.5) involved guiding the administrative team through the AI 4-D cycle. This process emphasized how to manage change and make shared, prioritized decisions. The assistant superintendent, as the AI facilitator, prepared the event and used one of the summer contract days in July for the AI event.

The summer events included reviewing building discipline data, identifying strengths, defining discipline codes, creating behavior matrices, determining classroom management training, and defining roles and expectations for teachers and for office referrals, and conducting research on responses to student behaviors. The building principals realized the value in the AI 4-D cycle and that simulating the AI 4-D cycle with their own building staff meant involving teachers in a collaborative, decision-making process. They wanted their staff to go through the same process having conversations and discussion on and determining meaning of terms like "horseplay" or "conduct-not defined" so they too, could come to common agreement and buy-in on how student behaviors and responses were to be managed.

The momentum of conversations and the energy of the building administrators grew throughout the day as they prioritized their efforts. The building administrators immediately began to prepare for Step 4 (Table 6.5), sharing the change and decision-making process with their staff. A couple of principals were hesitant about their abilities to lead their staff through the AI 4-D cycle, so principals from other buildings paired up and co-facilitated the process with each other, where School 1 scheduled the AI 4-D cycle two mornings and School 2 scheduled the AI 4-D cycle two afternoons.

Step 5 (Table 6.5) called for regularly scheduled monthly two-hour administrative meetings focused on leadership development. They shared progress on student discipline action plans created by their staff and reinforced the idea of unity (one voice for elementary; and one voice for secondary grades 6–12) on the bigger ideas such as defining discipline entry codes and responses to behaviors, creating positive classroom environments, and determining school-wide behaviors.

Monitoring progress on action plans, reflecting on changes in principal behaviors, and planning staff development revolved around the student discipline topic for the year. The process and conversations made a difference not only for the building level administrators but also for their staff. Principals reported their staff feeling empowered, trusted, and being held accountable for the co-constructed action plan. There was a sense of "us" shared from one of the buildings where the staff felt supported for the first time by the building principal. The staff reported one principal's demeanor had changed; he was more open, approachable, and constantly talked about the action plan and was enthusiastic to share progress and changes he was seeing, especially where more teacher-to-teacher interactions were focused on preventative student behavior measures and development of social and emotional skills.

The goal for the district administration was to help develop leadership through collaborative efforts and shared decision-making by focusing on a common topic of inquiry, student behaviors and discipline. At first, some of the administrators were in attendance based on mere compliance, but once they discovered the value of reviewing building and district student discipline data, sharing time-consuming discipline experiences, and learning about disparities among their own building practices they knew the co-created action plan was beginning to have merit; they looked forward to moving to the next step of determining what the literature or research said about student behaviors, and later on sharing the AI 4-D cycle as a tool and opportunity for collaboration, collective action planning, and direction with their buildings' staff.

The concept of leadership development continues in Chapters 7 and 8. Both chapters provide ways leadership influences student learning. Chapter 7 provides opportunity for administrators to work directly with teachers to improve effectiveness in the classroom as well as assist with the implementation of the AI 4-D cycle. Chapter 7 stems from Priority 2 (Table 6.4) teacher collaboration—bringing more cohesion among teachers in departments/teacher teams that were a collective instructional effort using data-driven decisions. Chapter 8, derived from Priority 3 (Table 6.4), meeting the needs of teachers by providing meaningful staff development also provided another way leadership influences student learning where strategies promote teachers working collaboratively to improve practices (Grissom et al., 2021). The AI 4-D cycle was used to bring innovation and shared decision-making to meet staff needs in multiple ways district-wide.

References

Grissom, J. A., Egalite, A. J., & Lindsay, C. A. (2021). How principals affect students and schools: A systematic synthesis of two decades of research. *The Wallace Foundation*. http://www.wallacefoundation.org/principalsynthesis

Poll Everywhere. (n.d.). Instant poll voting on smartphones. Retrieved August 13, 2022, from https://www.polleverywhere.com/smartphone-web-voting

7

Playbook for Scenario 3—developing a model teacher team

Topic or focus of inquiry—how can the high school English department become a model teacher team, more cohesive and focused on improving student learning?

The Playbook for Scenario 3 centers around the topic of developing a model high school English teacher team/PLC focused on working together and improving student learning. This chapter uses the same format as seen in the previous two chapters. The appreciative inquiry (AI) 4-D cycle steps and descriptions, the strengths-based questions used to guide the 4-D cycle discussions and sample responses are provided. The action plan and a summary of the process follow the destiny phase.

Participants in Scenario 3 involved 14 teachers who comprised the high school English department/PLC and two special education teachers who co-taught with the English teachers. One of the district assistant superintendents, facilitated the two-day AI 4-D cycle with an assistant principal as co-facilitator. A two-day agenda can be located in Chapter 9. The district arranged for substitute teachers. The Playbook for Scenario 3 asks, how can our high school English department/PLC become a model teacher team, more cohesive and focused on improving student learning?

The purpose for using the AI 4-D cycle was to help bring a decision-making framework to the group that would help procedurally in accomplishing tasks, and one that could lead the group toward a more positive mindset, that used strengths-based language. The initial AI summit was held off campus at the district's conference center in a classroom.

DOI: 10.4324/9781003350804-7

The four steps in the AI 4-D process are provided with guiding questions and sample responses. The past stories and connections from the discovery phase (Table 7.1) helped create a readiness for the future when imagining what was possible for their teacher team (Table 7.2). The design phase (Table 7.3) bridges the best from past experiences and what is valued with possibilities for a desired future. The destiny phase (Table 7.4) focuses on how the participants determined what could make their desired future come true. The solutions-based AI 4-D cycle resulted in the development of an action plan as noted in Table 7.5 for implementing Priority 1: An intentional focus and collaborative effort to achieve consistency among teachers in assignment expectations, grading, and use of assessment data to help improve student learning, thus changing the teacher team's story or destiny. The chapter concludes with the logistics of the AI event, a summary of the AI 4-D process, and how sustaining the plan has continued beyond the initial priorities.

The AI 4-D cycle

Table 7.1 represents the four types of questions used in the discovery phase of the AI 4-D cycle when working with the 16 high school teachers: Someone who was influential on them becoming high school English teachers and the qualities that they admired in that person, describing high point experiences within their teacher team, what they valued, and wished for their teacher team. In Part B, they were asked to identify common themes and determine what was most valued and wished for their teacher team.

Table 7.2 details step two of the AI 4-D cycle, the dream phase. The first part asked the teachers to imagine future possibilities of what could be for their students and for their high school English/language arts department. They described the ideal classroom, what it would take for every student to find success, and what their teacher team looked like when performing at its best. The second part asked the teachers to review the data, identifying common phrases and themes, and vote on those most important to them. Once the results were visible, the teachers prioritized the results.

Table 7.3 is the third step in the AI 4-D cycle where the teachers were asked to create bold statements (vision statements) of an idealized future merging the best of what was valued from the discovery stage with the ideal future from the dream stage.

Table 7.4 shows step four, the destiny phase, in the AI 4-D cycle. The teachers were asked what it would take to make the dream happen, so the participants created an action plan that would address Priority 1.

Table 7.1 Creating the model teacher team: the AI 4-D cycle, discovery phase

Background	Description	Sample Questions Used to Guide the 4-D Cycle	Sample Responses
Topic	Area of focus for change, innovation:	How can we as administrators help our building teacher teams/PLCs be more productive with greater focus on student learning?	
Participants	Who needs to be involved in the process?	Participants: A high school English/Language Arts department/PLC that consists of 14 teachers and two (inclusionary) special education teachers, One facilitator—district assistant superintendent, and One assistant or co-facilitator—high school assistant building principal.	

(continued)

Background	Description	Sample Questions Used to Guide the 4-D Cycle	Sample Responses
Steps in the AI 4-D cycle	Description	Sample Questions used to Guide the 4-D Cycle	Sample Responses
1. Discovery (Roles)	Part A: Share stories (the best from the past) to discover strengths, values, and wishes.	Describe the person who was most influential on you becoming an English teacher.	**Most Influential:** • My mother–an avid reader who was in multiple book clubs who would go to the library to do research on the author's background and on the settings for the novel (before Google). • My middle school English teacher who spent the time (a complete nine-weeks) on just two novels by Charles Dickens where I felt like we got to know the author and his style of writing). • A college literature professor— the expertise and passion in the storytelling on the background of authors and the settings for their novels or the explanations of the poems' meanings—the professor always had that hook of interest that engaged me in the class. • An author I met who inspired me. She talked nonstop at a book signing about a teacher that had encouraged her to write historical fiction.

| 1. Discovery (Roles) | Part A: Share stories (the best from the past) to discover strengths, values, and wishes. | What were the qualities that you admired in that person? | **Qualities that you Admire:**

• Humor.
• Relates well with students.
• Flexible, organized, and communicates well.
• Great work ethic.
• Clear and high expectations.
• Has patience and empathy.
• Kindness and compassion. |
| 1. Discovery (Roles) | Part A: Share stories (the best from the past) to discover strengths, values, and wishes. | Describe a high point experience where you were most proud to be a member of a team or of this high school English department/PLC. Who was involved? What was happening? | **High Point Experiences with Dept/PLC:**

• Building positive relationships as we worked on a unit that involved the Great American Read where the community was invited to see student exhibits.
• Recognition from administration for a job well done by our department at a school-wide staff meeting.
• When we found out that 25% of our students received a "5" on the AP exam—we went out for dinner one evening to celebrate.
• When we held Bard's [Shakespeare's] Birthday Bash for the whole school. |

(continued)

Background	Description	Sample Questions Used to Guide the 4-D Cycle	Sample Responses
1. Discovery (Roles)	Part A: Share stories (the best from the past) to discover strengths, values, and wishes.	What were the characteristics that made the high point experience one of the best?	**Characteristics:** • Learning that success forces you to grow and collaborate with others. • Structured opportunity to positively impact students. • Critical thinkers when we are open to ideas. • When we look for solutions.
1. Discovery (Roles)	Part A: Share stories (the best from the past) to discover strengths, values, and wishes.	What do you value most about your teacher team?	**Value Most:** • They are supportive. • Enjoy their friendship. • That they were student-oriented & professional. • Positive attitudes. • Work ethic was great. • They helped set the mood for the day. • Trust each other when you say you will do something, then it gets done. • Willing to help each other.

1. Discovery (Roles)	Part A: Share stories (the best from the past) to discover strengths, values, and wishes.	What three wishes do you have for your high school English department/PLC?	**Wishes:** • For everyone to value our meeting time. • Feel like we accomplish something when we meet/have goals. • Inclusiveness/feel like I belong/valued. • Discuss what works with student behaviors, absenteeism, incomplete work. • Continuity in course expectations among common courses. • Sharing with the new teachers.
1. Discovery (Roles)	Part B: Identify the themes and determine what's most valued, best practices, strengths	• Review the data and highlight or color code repeated phrases or put in a spreadsheet. • List most common phrases on big chart paper; review the data for success factors, discuss and vote on those most valued by the individuals. • Post votes (e.g., 3 dots to each person or use a conference live voting system with clicker/smartphones).	**Themes:** • Value positive, professional relationships. • Working with each other toward a common goal/shared vision. • Respect and honesty. • High expectations from all. • Foster student improvement and high quality, meaningful learning.

Table 7.2 Creating the model teacher team: the AI 4-D cycle, dream phase

Steps in the AI 4-D cycle	Description	Sample Questions Used to Guide the 4-D Cycle	Sample Responses
2. Dream (Discuss possible plays for the game)	Part A. Imagine future possibilities of what could be.	Review the Discovery Part B: What three wishes do you have for your teacher team (the HS English/Language Arts department/PLC)? And imagine what the ideal HS English/Language Arts department/PLC could be.	**3 Wishes** • Accomplish something real during PLC. • High expectations for students including their behaviors. • Willingness to share resources and strategies with one another. • Unified on beliefs and practices. • Concrete, specific goals for PLC. • Time for reteaching and sharing one-on-one. • Build positive relationships with each other. • Build positive relationships with students. • Volunteer ideas to help each other more often.
2. Dream (Discuss possible plays for the game)	Part A. Imagine future possibilities of what could be.	What would your classroom look like if every student in your class experienced success? What would it take to make that happen?	**For Every Student to Experience Success/What will it Take?** • No more excuses. • Specific professional development for English teachers. • Function as a cohesive unit and share individual lessons. • Only meaningful assignments. • Foster student achievement.

			• Focus on state assessment tested indicators/objectives (performance level descriptors). • Recognize that students don't all learn the same way and learn to connect with those struggling. • Students who could figure something out and make own improvements to their work. **Describe the Ideal Classroom—Impossible to Possible** • Students are engaged, responsive. • Students who could engage in real discussions over the materials. • Students who had a desire to learn • Students who were excited to be in your class. • Students discovering new intellectual passions. • Able to see the big picture. • Everyone engaged and staying on task. • Homework completed. • Excitement and smiling faces. • No discipline issues. • Good attendance. • Students showed personal desire to learn. • Students gave their best, working together and motivated, self-guided, stayed on task.
2. Dream (Discuss possible plays for the game)	Part A. Imagine future possibilities of what could be.	Describe what your classroom would look like on Thursday morning if the impossible were possible.	

(continued)

Steps in the AI 4-D cycle	Description	Sample Questions Used to Guide the 4-D Cycle	Sample Responses
2. Dream (Discuss possible plays for the game)	Part A. Imagine future possibilities of what could be.	Imagine your teacher team performing at its best. Describe what your English/Language Arts department/PLC would look like at Friday morning's meeting if the impossible were possible. How would the teacher team be interacting and operating?	**Teacher Team Performing at its Best:** • Have discussions over assignments to meet the needs of students. • Meaningful reward system for students who do well. • Functioned as a cohesive unit/dept. • Everything was considered innovative and fun with ways that motivated students. • Go below the surface and be able to teach depth of knowledge—having real conversations over literature/readings. • Knew our student's strengths & weaknesses to improve student learning. • We appreciated each other's strengths. • Shared lessons and teaching strategies. • We were operating on the same page—had calibration on grading/expectations on assignments that were common–Jr. Research Paper.

| 2. Dream (Discuss possible plays for the game) | Part B. Identify the themes, and determine what's most valued, best practices, strengths | • Review the data and highlight or color code repeated phrases or put in a spreadsheet.
• List most common phrases on big chart paper; review the data for success factors discuss and vote on those most valued by the individuals.
• Post votes (e.g., 3 dots to each person or use a conference live voting system with clicker/smartphones).
• Options for clarification are to review results through wish or dream statements (e.g., create a video, act out a skit, draw a mural or metaphor, write a story/poem, song) before writing vision statements. | After review of data, grouping data, and voting the themes included:
• Priority 4: Ability to inspire, promote learning, and engage students with opportunity to create lifelong learners.
• Priority 5: Make personal connections with students.
• Priority 2: High standards for all students.
• Priority 3: Help all students find success.
• Priority 1—most votes: An intentional focus and collaborative effort to achieve consistency among teachers in assignment expectations, grading, and use of assessment data to help improve student learning.
• Priority 6: Create a behaviors/rewards system for students. |

(continued)

Table 7.3 Creating the model teacher team: the AI 4-D cycle, design phase

Steps in the AI 4-D cycle	Description	Sample Questions Used to Guide the 4-D Cycle	Sample Responses
3. Design (Game Plan)	Create bold statements (vision statements) of an idealized future merging the best of what is valued from the discovery stage with the ideal future from the dream stage (Based on priorities in the Discovery and Dream phases, prioritize and gain consensus of what should be).	Ask, does the design use all the most important factors from the lists created in the discovery and dream phases? Address the four priority Ps when creating the vision statements: • people (who we are and who are we when we are at our best), • purpose (our goal), • principles (what we value and believe), and • practices (the world we want to live in and create together). This includes the vision, purpose, and commitment along with other items listed that help define the preferred future.	• We are lifelong learners; we love to learn ourselves—reading and writing are our passion. We want to instill that in others. • To inspire. • Be purposeful and intentional learning. • Work respectfully as colleagues. • Hard work pays off. • Committed and cohesive unit. • Want engaged and dedicated students.

	The bold, vision statements:		
3. Design (Game Plan)		Our vision for the ideal teacher team (HS English Language Arts/PLC):	**Our vision for the ideal teacher team (HS English Language Arts/PLC):** Our actions demonstrate that we work as one cohesive unit with a vision focused on instilling a lifelong love for learning specifically in the areas of reading, writing, and analysis.
3. Design (Game Plan)		Our Purpose:	**Our Purpose:** We help inspire world class students who are successful, inquisitive, and hungry for meaningful dialogue on materials read and written in and out of the classroom.
3. Design (Game Plan)		Our Committed Working Relationships:	**Our Committed Working Relationships:** We are committed to creating a safe and open environment that is honest where all members can be equally recognized, engaged, and involved in meaningful dialogue based on the continuous improvement of our students' state assessment scores and ACT scores. We commit to the collective agreements as established within our HS English/Language Arts department/PLC.

Table 7.4 Creating the model teacher team: the AI 4-D cycle, destiny phase

Steps in the AI 4-D cycle	Description	Sample Questions Used to Guide the 4-D Cycle	Sample Responses
4. Destiny (The Playbook)	Create and commit to the action plan and to sustaining the plan, making it happen!	What will it take to make the dream come true? Create an action plan, a detailed plan outlining the steps to accomplish the goal(s) with an implementation timeline: address processes, people, resources that need to be in place, timelines, and celebration milestones. The action plan should answer the 4Ws + 2Hs: Who, What, Where, When, plus How and How much. The action plan should be written to include… • SMART goals, • Deadlines, • List of activities or tasks that need to be completed, • A visual so progress can be monitored and reviewed, reprioritized, celebrated; and • Your commitment to the task(s) or action(s). List three ways you can help contribute to achieving the plan.	In this example, the overall objective is stated. Table 7.5 shows the action plan for Priority 1, which includes two tasks and two goals. Priority 1: An intentional focus and collaborative effort to achieve consistency among teachers in assignment expectations, grading, and use of assessment data to help improve student learning. Priority 2: High standards for all students. Priority 3: Help all students find success.

Action plan

Table 7.5 is the first part of the action plan co-created by the 16 teachers as a part of the destiny phase in the AI 4-D cycle to address Priority 1. The objective is stated along with Task 1: Teachers will review student data to help guide and improve student learning.

Summary: Chapter 7 playbook for Scenario 3—developing a model teacher team

Logistics

The Playbook for Scenario 3 used the AI 4-D change method as a strengths-based process where the English department/PLC could practice becoming more productive with meeting time while collaboratively focusing on student learning. The 14 high school English teachers and two special education teachers participated in the two-day event. The district's assistant superintendent led the process and helped model the AI 4-D cycle for one of the high school assistant principals who would be assisting the teachers throughout the remainder of the school year. Also, the high school teachers were held accountable for the implementation of the action plans co-constructed in the destiny stage.

The facilitator knew in advance there would be 16 attendees from the high school, so two colors of sticky dots—yellow and blue, were randomly assigned to the name tags, thus two groups of eight people for later activities. The AI process is highly participatory. The participants worked in pairs, groups of 4, groups of 8, and as a whole group during the initial two-day AI 4-D cycle event. The members of the high school English department/PLC were welcomed and asked to share the title of a favorite childhood story or storybook. There was an agenda overview for the first day with an introduction to AI and to the AI 4-D cycle. Sample agendas are located in Chapter 9.

Attendees participated in establishing team norms or ground rules. The process for establishing team norms or ground rules was similar to the large groups with 120–130 participants (See Chapter 4). Sixteen teachers were divided into two groups based on the color of the sticky dot on their name tag—either the blue group or the yellow group. They were asked to self-manage with one person as recorder, who took notes on the large chart paper, and one person as reporter, who would share what had been discussed to both table groups; in this situation, the two table groups was equivalent to

Table 7.5 Creating the model teacher team: the AI 4-D cycle, Destiny phase action plan, Part 1

Action Plan–Part 1 Collaborative Efforts for English/Language Arts PLC to Improve Student Learning Using Student Data and Defining Exemplary Work

Overall Objective: Over the next year, the HS English/Language Arts Department/PLC will collectively make instructional decisions based on available data that can improve student learning to a level where 50% of the students are scoring in the Effective and/or Exemplary categories as measured by the Grade 11 English/Language Arts (ELA) 2021 state assessment. This would be a 19% increase in movement from the limited and basic categories.

Current Situation: The two most recent years for Grade 11 English/Language Arts State Assessment data are as follows:

Level: Yr	Limited (1)	Basic (2)	Effective (3)	Exemplary (4)
2018	14%	44%	32%	10%
2017	15%	41%	34%	10%

Priority 1: An intentional focus and collaborative effort to achieve consistency among teachers in assignment expectations, grading, and use of assessment data to help improve student learning.

Goal 1: The high school English/Language Arts Department/PLC will use the Grade 11 state English/Language Arts student assessment data available over the past two years to identify students' strengths and weaknesses on tested indicators to guide instruction to help meet the needs of all students, with the SMART goal of attaining a learning level where at least 50% of the students are scoring in the Effective and/or Exemplary categories on next year's state assessment.

Task 1: Teachers will review student data to help guide and improve student learning.

What Action Step Description	Who Person/Dept Responsible	When Begin Date	When Due Date	How Materials/ Resources Needed	How Much	Notes
Step 1: Organize grade 11 student ELA assessment data reports for review from past two years for each tested indicator overall for the ELA department, by teacher, by subgroups (e.g., male/female) highlighting in green the Effective 3s and Exemplary 4s levels; in yellow` the Basic 2s level, and in red the Limited 1s level.	District and building assessment coordinators; ELA Dept/PLC lead teacher	Aug 3	Aug 9	Paper copies of assessment results as well as electronic spreadsheets.		3 different meetings with discussions between building assessment coordinator and ELA Dept/PLC lead teacher to prepare for ELA Dept/PLC Data review meeting.

(continued)

Task 1: Teachers will review student data to help guide and improve student learning.

What Action Step Description	Who Person/Dept Responsible	When Begin Date	When Due Date	How Materials/ Resources Needed	How Much	Notes
Step 2: Meet to review data as the English/Language Arts Dept/PLC: Identify strengths and weaknesses for all grade 11 students by tested indicators and tell our "story" based on what we feel is working in the department as a whole that contributes to student success. Review data by teacher and prioritize list of strengths based on data (high to low); finish and bring to next meeting with evidence or examples.	Building assessment coordinator, ELA Dept/PLC lead teacher, ENG Dept/PLC members	Sept 15- early dismissal (1–3:30)		Paper copies of assessment results as well as electronic spreadsheets. Large chart paper / tablets. Markers/highlighters Time set aside: ½ day meeting. Team norms/ground rules paper to review.		1/2 day (1:00–3:30) ELA Dept/PLC staff development early dismissal Wednesday.

Share lists of strengths based on indicator data (high to low) and the evidence such as example assignments, student work, etc.	ELA Dept/PLC lead teacher, ENG Dept/PLC members	Sept 29 early dismissal (1–3:30)		Large chart paper/tablets. Markers/highlighters. Team norms/ground rules. Bring your list of strengths (high to low) and evidence of what's working with examples of assignments & student work for top four strengths.	Examples: Tone analysis with a *King Arthur* assignment—progression from rough to final draft with implementation of stronger writing techniques. Critical analysis of Hurston's novel, *Their Eyes Were Watching God*—essay reaches deeper and has higher order thinking skills using quotes and examples, asks students to dig deeper into the literary techniques.

(continued)

Task 1: Teachers will review student data to help guide and improve student learning.

What Action Step Description	Who Person/Dept Responsible	When Begin Date	When Due Date	How Materials/ Resources Needed	How Much	Notes
Step 3: Rank order performances on state data and identify at four tested indicators for department as a whole to focus on vertically at grades 9-10-11. Review and discuss what a Level 4: (Exemplary) looks like based on performance level descriptors.	ELA Dept/PLC lead teacher, ENG Dept/PLC members	Oct 13- early dismissal (1–3:30)		Copies of the standards tested by the state with performance level descriptors' document found at https:// ksassessments.org.		Example: Focus Area 1—Gr 10, Indicator 9: "Draw evidence from grades 9–10 literary or informational texts to support analysis, reflection, and research" (KAP ELA Target, 2018, p. 17).

Step 4: Review other formal data points: (e.g., NWEA Map tests for grades 9, 10; STAR testing; common assessments for grades 9, 10, 11, 12; ACT data) for strengths and weaknesses. Determine how each of the formal assessments can help address the top four areas as determined in Steps 2–3.	Building assessment coordinator, ELA Dept/PLC lead teacher, ENG Dept/PLC members	Oct 27- early dismissal (1–3:30)	Paper copies of assessment results as well as electronic spreadsheets. Large chart paper/tablets. Markers/highlighters. Time set aside: ½ day meeting. Team norms/ground rules paper to review.	1/2 day (1:00–3:30) ELA Dept/PLC staff development early dismissal Wednesday, much like the process in Step 2, looking for what contributes to student success.
Step 5: Determine what skills are needed for each of the four tested indicators (unpack, deconstruct the standards/tested indicators)	Secondary curriculum coordinator, ELA Dept/PLC lead teacher, ENG Dept/PLC members	Nov 2–3 Staff Development Days		Purpose—Deconstruct Standards: 1. Analyze the wording. 2. Rephrase the indicator in own words. 3. Create essential questions. 4. Write a progression—simple to more complex learning targets. 5. Check for same level of thinking/rigor.

(continued)

Task 1: Teachers will review student data to help guide and improve student learning.

What Action Step Description	Who Person/Dept Responsible	When Begin Date	When Due Date	How Materials/ Resources Needed	How Much	Notes
Step 6: Determine where skills are taught in various assignments (Review the assignments discussed in Step 2 where teachers discussed what was working or which assignments may have contributed to student success and compare and contrast with skills needed as identified in Step 5). Repeat for each of the four focus tested indicators. Determine which skills are missing based on the unpacking/ deconstructing charts to address.	Secondary curriculum coordinator, ELA Dept/PLC lead teacher, ENG Dept/PLC members	Nov 2–3 Staff Development Days		Bring copies of the standards tested by the state with performance level descriptors' document. Bring assignments you and/or your grade level(s) uses to address the four standards that are the focus for the state assessment. Curriculum maps. Team norms/ground rules paper to review.	$1,600 for substitutes.	Nov 2-district day. Nov 3-substitutes needed. Continued unpacking/ deconstructing process.

the whole group. Each table brainstormed ground rules or team norms; they had the option of passing. The reporter from each table group shared; then the two lists were merged into one set of ground rules or team norms. They agreed to abide by the rules whenever there was a meeting, and they agreed to post the ground rules or team norms visually during meetings. They also agreed that the ground rules or team norms could be revised at any time so long as the rules were agreed upon by the group. Again, it is important to stress that ground rules or team norms are visually displayed and reviewed prior to each meeting and sometimes reminded of the rules during meetings. The results, the team norms/ground rules are depicted in Chapter 4, Table 4.1 on the right side of the table.

The 4-Ds

The discovery phase asked the four standard types of AI questions that are shared through storytelling: a past, personal story; a high point or outstanding experience with the team or group; values or characteristics they value; and three wishes for a desired future. In pairs, the Scenario 3 participants were asked to describe the person who was most influential on them becoming a high school English teacher or teacher and the qualities that they admired in that person. The first two strengths-based questions used in the discovery phase were intentionally written to be focused on another person, rather than on the participant, to help with a few participants who were hesitant about attending the summit. Being able to share or talk about yourself can oftentimes be difficult.

They were also asked to describe a high point experience where they were most proud to be a member of a team or of this high school English department and detail what made that one of the best experiences. The pairs also asked each other what they valued about their teacher team and what three wishes they had for their teacher team.

At the table groups, each pair shared what they had heard from their partner. They discussed the commonalities and themes, creating a list of characteristics in people that had influenced them to become teachers, what they valued, and wishes that they had for their teacher team. The recorder at each table took notes and the reporters shared with the whole group. Once again, commonalities and themes were identified. Each person voted with a set of three sticky dots on the listed items that were of most value to them. Overall, the 16 teachers could see visually on the wall what was valued by the whole group.

The dream phase asked for participants to take the best of the past or current situation and wishes from the discovery phase and imagine future possibilities for the ideal or model teacher team that was focused on improving student learning. In pairs, they shared what their classroom would look like if every student experienced success, and what their classroom would look like on Thursday morning if the impossible were possible. They also imagined what their teacher team would look like if performing at its best and how they were interacting and operating. The process was repeated by sharing with the table group, taking notes on large chart paper, reviewing the data, highlighting or color-coding repeated phrases, identifying common themes, and reviewing the data for success factors.

After discussion, the top 3–5 areas were prioritized with each person voting on the ideas most valued. Next, the priorities were shared with the other table group where common themes were discussed, and priorities were again determined by voting. The top priorities were (a) an intentional focus and collaborative effort to achieve consistency among teachers in assignment expectations, grading, and use of assessment data to help improve student learning; (b) high standards for all students; and (c) helping all students find success. At this point, the priorities were clarified by writing a poem and drawing a metaphor before creating vision statements.

The design phase asked participants to create bold, vision statements defining who they are and where they want to be bridging the discovery and dream phases. The destiny phase asked them to operationalize the bold, vision statements by asking what it would take to make the vision statements happen when considering their priorities. An action plan was co-created and included Priority 1, which had two goals with two tasks and multiple action steps to be taken over the course of the next year. Participants were asked to commit to the action plan, to make the dream happen, realizing their future. Before leaving the AI 4-D two-day summit, the 16 teachers completed exit tickets and shared the most rewarding part of the event.

Sustaining the plan

The AI facilitator and the assistant principal held the high school teachers accountable for the implementation of the action plans co-created in the destiny stage, monitoring their progress toward a preferred future. Logistics of the meetings became very important to the teachers. They met in a different person's classroom each time and re-arranged the classroom furniture so they could meet in a variety of settings: Pairs, in four groups of four, or two groups of eight. The department head/lead teacher for the English department/PLC became the facilitator and kept the group focused on the task at hand, was the timekeeper, and reminded the group to review the ground rules from time to time. The group norms or ground rules were revised a couple of times and became more of a public agreement, putting friendships or conflict aside while meeting and working with each other for a greater purpose of staying focused on improving student learning.

Each time the department/PLC met, roles were assigned for recorder and reporter. The recorder took notes that were visible to the group (e.g., using large chart paper/markers, marker board, the interactive board, projected computer screen). The reporter restated and reaffirmed what was said, decided, agreed upon based on the notes visually displayed.

It was recommended and agreed upon by the teachers that a cup be available at each meeting with the names on strips of paper or craft sticks of the 16 teachers attending the meetings from the English/language arts department/PLC. The facilitator, after the first three meetings, was the lead teacher/department head who drew two names out of the basket during each meeting. The first name drawn became the recorder at the next meeting, and the second name drawn would be the reporter. The current meeting's recorder put the agreed upon information in the notes, and the current reporter sent out the email reminder with 48-hour notice prior to the next meeting. The process for appointing recorder and reporter repeated itself throughout the year.

With 10 minutes left before adjourning each meeting, the facilitator asked for input and guidance in determining the next meeting time and location (PLC time was already built into the district's calendar during early release days) with a focus, specifically on what they wanted to get accomplished at the next meeting and how this would be accomplished along with any specific materials/resources that may be needed so teachers could come prepared.

When the action plan for the destiny phase was completed, the celebration occurred at an August meeting after reviewing the past spring state assessment data. The AI 4-D cycle now repeats itself based on the next question the high school English/language arts department/PLC establishes as inquiry. The next steps came quite naturally, when they began to ask:

> How do we know that a student has mastered a specific skill or tested indicator? And, how can we get that information to us in an easy-to-use format?
> How are students given a second chance to succeed?
> How can we minimize disruptive student behaviors that happen weekly and even daily with some students?
> How can we help students improve their writing abilities?

Now familiar with change process, the teachers are empowered for success; they can facilitate their own AI 4-D cycle inquiry. The teachers have become a more cohesive unit with productive meetings focused on improving teaching processes and student learning; it empowered the team, knowing they were able to establish results-oriented meetings and achieve some of their goals.

Some of their comments were promising for continued use of the AI process with its 4-D cycle as they began Year 2:

> I think everyone is more receptive to everyone's ideas.
> Being positive is in the air—refreshing.
> I'm glad we've had the chance to prioritize our next steps and direction this year.
> I've actually gotten to know several of you better.
> We don't always agree, but we can leave with a concrete product.
> I have a positive feeling; I'm much more hopeful.
> There's a lot of promise with this process.

The AI 4-D change model helped one high school assistant principal develop leadership skills facilitating the collaboration efforts of the teacher team/PLC, engaging with the teachers as they interacted on instructional practices, and ensuring amicable relationships which led to a more positive, cooperative environment. Chapter 8 focuses on developing leadership skills addressing district-wide, meaningful staff development opportunities.

Reference

KAP ELA Target. (2018). Assessment Development Guide Educator Resource English Language Arts: Grade 10. https://ksassessments.org/sites/default/files/documents/ELA/ELA_Grade_10_Assessment_Development_Guide.pdf

8

Playbook for Scenario 4—district-wide meaningful professional development

Topic or focus of inquiry—how can our district inspire, encourage, and support classroom teachers through meaningful professional learning experiences?

This chapter, The Playbook for Scenario 4, focuses on how districts can provide meaningful professional learning options that inspire, encourage, and support classroom teachers. The impetus for using the appreciative inquiry (AI) 4-D cycle for meaningful professional learning and staff development derived from Chapter 5, Priority 2 (Table 5.2) meeting the needs of teachers in our buildings by providing meaningful staff development, has provided yet another way leadership influences staff and students.

Scenario 4 helps increase principal leadership capacity by modeling and assisting building administrators where they had opportunity to develop positive, working relationships with teachers, manage change more effectively through shared decision-making via the AI 4-D rapid, change model, and then held teachers accountable through the co-constructed action plans.

Co-creating a meaningful district-wide staff development plan included the district administrative team, approximately 350 staff, plus 40 special education teachers who were assigned to and worked in the district from the special education cooperative. Every licensed employee PreK-12 was asked to complete the discovery and dream phases of the AI 4-D cycle through

DOI: 10.4324/9781003350804-8

an online survey. Basic demographic questions were asked such as male/ female, years of teaching experience in total, years of teaching experience in the district, and at which levels and subjects. The discovery phase four initial questions were asked in the survey in relation to staff trainings/in-services: A memorable past story about a professional learning experience, a best training experience or high point experience in a training session, what is most valued in professional learning experiences, wishes for the ideal professional learning experience, and imagining what the ideal professional learning experiences could be if the impossible were possible.

By building administrator recommendation, a district-wide professional development committee (PDC) was formed with two representatives from each building and one special education teacher who represented the 40 special education teachers. They participated in phases three and four of the AI 4-D cycle. One of the assistant superintendents was the AI facilitator, with two building principals as co-facilitators, who prepared the agendas and set up the district's conference center room with supplies and food. A sample one-day agenda can be found in Chapter 9.

The Playbook for Scenario 4 asks, how can our district inspire, encourage, and support classroom teachers through meaningful professional learning experiences? The purpose for using the AI 4-D cycle was to activate a change process that would help inspire, encourage, and support classroom teachers through meaningful staff development district-wide. The online survey served as a vehicle to hear the voices from all staff. The online survey data, which included questions from the AI 4-D cycle discovery and dream phases, were shared and analyzed by the district PDC and building principals.

Survey questions are provided in Table 8.1. The data helped create a readiness for the future when imagining what could be possible for ideal staff development options. After an analysis of the data, the district's PDC then participated in the design phase which bridges the best from past experiences with what is valued and considered to be possibilities for a desired future. The district-wide PDC group was also instrumental in the destiny phase participating in collective action planning efforts, co-constructing a desired future with multiple options for meaningful staff development.

The same format has been used as seen in the previous Playbooks for Scenarios 1, 2, and 3 in Chapters 5, 6, and 7 where the AI 4-D cycle steps and strengths-based questions used to guide the discussions throughout the 4-D cycle with sample responses are provided. In addition, a summary of the process with a follow up, detailing the sustainability of the change model are included. The AI 4-D cycle is detailed in Table 8.1.

Table 8.1 Meaningful staff development: the AI 4-D cycle: discovery, dream, destiny, and design phases

Steps	Description	Sample Questions Used to Guide the 4-D Cycle	Sample Responses
Topic	Area of focus for change, innovation:	How can our district inspire, encourage, and support classroom teachers through meaningful professional learning experiences?	
Participants	Who needs to be involved in the process?	All licensed staff including special educators from the special education cooperative were included in the discovery phase (390 licensed staff).	
		Two representatives from each building were involved in the other phases, plus one special education teacher (21 representatives).	
		The professional development committee (PDC) of 21 and building principals were involved in the data analysis from the discovery phase and then participated in the design and destiny phases.	

(continued)

Steps	Description	Sample Questions Used to Guide the 4-D Cycle	Sample Responses
1. Discovery (Roles)	Part A: Share stories (the best from the past) to discover strengths, values, and wishes.	Online questionnaire:	Discovery: All staff had the opportunity to complete the online questionnaire.
		Part 1: About You.	
		Part 2: Discovery questions.	
		Part 3: Rank order topics you feel are most necessary.	
		Part 4: Preferred learning format(s).	
1. Discovery (Roles)	Part A: Share stories (the best from the past) to discover strengths, values, and wishes.	The most effective professional development learning experience that I have ever participated in was: (be specific—describe the setting, time of day, size of group, and what you were doing).	Most effective: • Hands-on activities, 10-15 people in a group, activity that relates to our classroom/grade level. • Visiting other schools and classrooms in action in my field—anytime—especially those using centers or only computer learning! • In the Summer mornings, Kagan workshops. I always got something I could use, and it was delivered in an entertaining relaxing setting.

- Breakout sessions with choice like I experienced at a national conference.
- During the day with teachers who are devoted to teaching what I teach at the same grade level. Most effective because we all had the same focus.
- The class was a "make it take it" style for center ideas in the classroom. It was called a breakout session. I would love to see this done for intervention group ideas. Maybe ½ day.
- I appreciated going to other schools during a time when their school was in session and seeing how they did guided reading lessons and centers with their students. I found this to be most helpful.
- Developing classroom discipline skills, workshop had a multitude of methods used to present material along with ample time for discussion and feedback.

(continued)

Steps	Description	Sample Questions Used to Guide the 4-D Cycle	Sample Responses
1. Discovery (Roles)	Part A: Share stories (the best from the past) to discover strengths, values, and wishes.	What were the characteristics that made the professional learning experience most effective?	Characteristics of the best professional learning experiences: • University courses/workshops are relevant and effective by being hands-on, I was able to leave with assignments, worksheets, etc. already created and ready to use in my classroom. • The speaker engaged everyone, by allowing participants to practice some of the methods she was discussing. We moved around, discussed, practiced, and she had ideas to cover reading in all subjects. • Small groups, time for discussions. • The district used to do breakout sessions during in-service. I felt those were the best as the individual had some control over their learning. • Breakout sessions—especially where there are topics that are relevant.

1. Discovery (Roles)	Part A: Share stories (the best from the past) to discover strengths, values, and wishes.	What do you value most when time is designated as professional learning, staff development, or in-service days?
		Most valued: • Hands-on—keep me moving and learning. • Engaged. • Choice in sessions. • Summer for credit using our ideas to accomplish what we need—from online resources that we have found / Florida online resources, Pinterest ideas. • Humor and fun. • Relevant. • Working on what's important to our English department and keeping everyone in attendance and focused on common goals. • Choices and more on ideas for integration of technologies. • Small setting where we actually got to practice the skills that were presented - like our Kagan training. • Hands-on learning works best for me. • Appropriate application time—when we are learning about a new curriculum or topic, we need to be given time to learn how to use it, work with it and apply it to our classrooms.

(continued)

Steps	Description	Sample Questions Used to Guide the 4-D Cycle	Sample Responses
1. Discovery	Part A: Share stories (the best from the past) to discover strengths, values, and wishes.	If you could design the ideal professional learning experience, what would you wish for or what would it look like?	The ideal professional learning experience design: • Make it hands-on and directed by peers. • Sessions taught by the experts/more experienced teachers. • Where we get to choose four session topics throughout the day. • Time to work with members of our department who have common goals. • Emphasis on Technology, Technology, and Technology! • More teambuilding and classbuilding ideas—what are others doing? • No more all-day lecturers with constant sitting and listening. It is too hard on a person to have to sit and listen. • I suggest learning about something in the morning and then putting it to work in the afternoon developing it or discussing it to build upon it to make it relevant to our teaching in the afternoon.

			• Time to design lessons and be creative; not always about data. • Choice in sessions. • Summer, for credit using our ideas to accomplish what we need—from online resources that we have found/Pinterest ideas. • Humor and fun. • Fieldtrips.
1. Discovery	Part B. Identify the themes and determine what's most valued, best practices, strengths.	Review the data and highlight or color code repeated phrases or put in a spreadsheet.	Themes: • Breakout sessions. • Choice. • Hands-on. • Practical and applicable. • Relevant. • Peer to peer observations, conversations. • Collaboration time. • Technology. • Learn from peers. • Varied formats–breakouts, choice, summer paid to attend, for credit.
		List most common phrases on big chart paper; review the data for success factors discuss and vote on those most valued by the individuals.	
		Post votes (e.g., three dots to each person or use a conference live voting system with clicker/smartphones).	

(continued)

Steps	Description	Sample Questions Used to Guide the 4-D Cycle	Sample Responses
1. Dream (Possible Plays)	Part A. Imagine future possibilities of what could be.	What three wishes do you have for the ideal professional learning experiences for yourself? For your teacher team? For your school? And your school district?	Three Wishes: • Take all the themes and make it happen so we have a variety of choices in format and dates/times including summers academies with pay. • TICs (Technology Instructional Coaches). • Relevant. • Engaging. • Choices with multiple formats.
2. Dream (Possible Plays)	Part A. Imagine future possibilities of what could be.	Imagine the ideal professional learning experience. Describe what the next professional learning experience would look like In-service Day, October 11 (Columbus Day) if the impossible were possible. What are the teachers doing and saying? How are they interacting?	Describe the Ideal Professional Learning Experience—Impossible to Possible: Professional learning at its best: A variety of formats/times/styles: • Our own designed, for graduate credit courses: (e.g. Happy Appy Classroom—aligning apps to curriculum standards); Teaching Reading Cross-curricular Style). • Summer Staff Academies—teachers paid and teachers as facilitators get double pay (Centered on Make It & Take It for Centers; Outdoor Classroom at the River).

			• Just in Time workshops (Deconstructing, or Unpacking the standards; Data-driven Dialogue Day—it's all about Focus, not Hocus Pocus). • Our own district-wide, mini one-day conference modeled after national conferences with lots of choices, breakout sessions taught by our own (called the Big Cat Conference). • Offer help to those who want to get their reading specialists or ESOL endorsement.	After review of data, grouping data, and voting the themes included: • Priority 1—tied: Big Cat Conference—breakout sessions with teachers teaching peers. • Priority 1—tied: Create our own university graduate credit courses. • Priority 2: Summer Staff Academies. • Priority 3: Just in Time learning. • Priority 6: Reading specialists. • Priority 7: ESOL endorsements. • Priority 4: Technology Instructional Coaches and evidence-based strategists. • Priority 5: Late start/early dismissals for collaboration time.
2. Dream (Possible Plays)	Part B. Identify the themes, and determine what's most valued, best practices, strengths.	Post votes (e.g., three dots to each person or use a conference live voting system with clicker/smartphones). Options for clarification are to review results through wish or dream statements (e.g. create a video, act out a skit, draw a mural or metaphor, write a story/poem, song) before writing vision statements.	

(continued)

Steps	Description	Sample Questions Used to Guide the 4-D Cycle	Sample Responses
3. Design (Game Plan)	Create bold statements (vision statements) of an idealized future merging the best of what is valued from the discovery stage with the ideal future from the dream stage.	Ask, does the design use all the most important factors from the lists created in the discovery and dream phases?	Our vision for the ideal professional learning experience: • Our actions show we offer multi-format, highly effective training experiences that are timely, of current concern, and based on staff feedback.
	Prioritize and gain consensus of what should be.	Address the 4 Priority Ps: people (who we are and who are we when we are at our best); purpose (our goal), principles (what we value and believe), and practices (the world we want to live in and create together). This includes our vision, purpose, belief, and commitment along with other items listed that help define the preferred future.	
		Our Vision:	

| 3. Design (Game Plan) | Create bold statements (vision statements) of an idealized future merging the best of what is valued from the discovery stage with the ideal future from the dream stage. | Our Purpose: | Our Purpose: • We give voice to the interests and professional learning needs of staff, holding each other accountable for sustaining a collaborative and continuous improvement culture. |
| | Prioritize and gain consensus of what should be. | | |

(continued)

Steps	Description	Sample Questions Used to Guide the 4-D Cycle	Sample Responses
3. Design (Game Plan)	Create bold statements (vision statements) of an idealized future merging the best of what is valued from the discovery stage with the ideal future from the dream stage.	Our Belief and Commitment:	Our Belief and Commitment: • We believe all staff can be equally recognized, engaged, and involved in meaningful professional learning focused on student learning and the well-being of self. We commit to providing the learning experiences and support that leads to effective teaching, collaborative learning and inquiry, and improved student learning.
	Prioritize and gain consensus of what should be.		
4. Destiny (The Playbook)	Create and commit to the action plan and to sustaining the plan, making it happen!	What will it take to make the dream come true? Create an action plan, a detailed plan outlining the steps to accomplish the goal(s) with an implementation timeline: address processes, people, resources that need to be in place,	• In this example, the overall objective is stated. Typically, action plans are then written for the top 3 priorities. This example, Table 8.2, shows the action plan for the top three priorities: 1a, 1b, and 2. • **Overall Objective:** Over the next year, the PDC will make professional learning decisions based on the voice and prioritized needs of district staff by accomplishing at least three of the priorities this year.

- **Current Situation:** This year has five in-service/staff development days. Two at the beginning of the year, prior to school and three days throughout the year: On Columbus Day, Martin Luther King, Jr. Day, and Good Friday. A reallocation of funds may help with several priorities being accomplished.
- Priority 1—tied: a) simulate a national conference with breakout sessions for all staff district-wide, to be known as the Big Cat Conference and b) design university credit courses/workshops tailored to staff interests.

See the Action Plan, Table 8.2 Big Cat Conference) and Univ. Credit Workshops for the goals and tasks for Priority 1a, 1b, and Priority 2.

- Priority 2: Summer Academies—apply for your area of learning/activity time during the summer.
- Priority 3: Just in Time learning workshops—last minute, basic information how to enter grades, how to prepare for the state assessment.

---

timelines, and celebration milestones. The action plan should answer the 4Ws + 2Hs: Who, What, Where, When, plus How and How much. The action plan should be written to include…

- SMART goals,
- Deadlines,
- List of activities or tasks that need to be completed,
- A visual, so progress can be monitored and reviewed, reprioritized, celebrated; and
- Your commitment to the task(s) or action(s). List three ways you can help contribute to achieving the plan.

The AI 4-D cycle

Table 8.1 shows the four phases in the AI 4-D cycle. Guiding questions and sample responses are provided. The results show how the PDC was able to plan and prioritize meaningful and innovative district-wide professional learning experiences.

Action plan

Table 8.2 shows the action plan co-created during the AI 4-D cycle destiny phase to address Priority 1a: Simulate a national conference type professional learning day that included choice in learning topics with multiple breakout sessions where staff were teaching staff; Priority 1b: Organize and create graduate courses/workshops for credit taught by own staff/administrators to be held on school district campus that addressed their needs; and Priority 2: Organize and create Summer Staff Academy workshops where teachers were paid to focus on the delivery and creation of general education interventions (GEIs) and instructional strategies that were evidenced-based, providing a more student-centered approach to learning.

Summary: Chapter 8 playbook for Scenario 4—district-wide meaningful professional development

Logistics

This chapter, The Playbook for Scenario 4—district-wide, meaningful professional development, is focused on how to support classroom teachers through meaningful professional learning experiences. An online survey was designed so the voices of all licensed staff could be heard. Questions asked in the survey were those asked in Table 8.1 during the discovery and dream phases.

The district-wide PDC consisted of 20 staff representing all buildings along with one special education teacher representative. The assistant superintendent with help from the PDC, created the initial survey that was posted online for all licensed staff PreK-12. The same 21 people participated in the AI summit, along with the building administrators. The AI 4-D cycle used a facilitator, the assistant superintendent, to help the PDC learn the process and hold them accountable for the implementation of the action plans co-constructed in the destiny phase.

Table 8.2 The action plan created during the AI 4-D cycle destiny phase

Action Plan Meaningful Professional Learning Experiences
Overall Objective: Over the next year, the PDC will make professional learning decisions based on the voice and prioritized wishes from the online survey all licensed staff completed, by accomplishing at least the top priorities: 1a, 1b, and 2 over the next year.
Current Situation: This year has five in-service/staff development days. Two at the beginning of the year and three days throughout the year: On Columbus Day, Martin Luther King, Jr. Day, and Good Friday. A reallocation of funds may help with several priorities being accomplished.
Priority 1a: Simulate a national conference type professional learning day that includes choice and control in learning topics through multiple breakout sessions where staff are teaching staff.
Goal 1: All staff will have the opportunity to participate in an in-service day (Martin Luther King, Jr district in-service day) designed primarily by teachers and taught by teachers or with topic relevancy as noted in the staff survey results.

Task 1: Create a district-wide Big Cat Conference based on teaching staff Priority 1.

What Action Step Description	Who Person/Dept. Responsible	When Begin Date	When Due Date	How Materials/ Resources Needed	How Much	Notes
Step 1: Create breakout proposal forms and advertise in each building; PDC reps solicit between 7 and 10 proposals (60 or 90 minute workshops from their buildings).	PDC members; principals; Ass't. Supt. & her secretary	Sept 27	Nov 30	Proposal forms.		PDC organizational meeting.

(continued)

Task 1: Create a district-wide Big Cat Conference based on teaching staff Priority 1.

What Action Step Description	Who Person/ Dept. Responsible	When Begin Date	When Due Date	How Materials/ Resources Needed	How Much	Notes
Step 2: Coordinate organizational meetings with other district services/ departments.	Ass't. Supt. with Food Service; High School A Principal, Tech Director & Tech Staff; Assistant Principals	Nov 18	Dec 15	Assistant Principals were in charge acquiring 3–5 drawing prizes donated by community partnerships (e.g., gift cards to Target, restaurants, spa, tech item donated by Walmart).		Organizational meetings-location at HS A; work with food service, lunch on site at HS on Jan 17 for 425 people; prepare tech staff on wireless capacity.
Step 3: Review Proposals & Make Recommendations for Breakout sessions; Submit to Ass't. Supt.	PDC members, Principals	Dec 1	Dec 15			At buildings.
Step 4: Set up draft schedule for the day and logistics for the Big Cat Conference.	PDC members Ass't. Supt., secretary	Dec 17- 7:30a.m.- 9:00a.m.	Dec 17	District Office; Block 1 –subs for HS staff.	$72	PDC meeting before school.

Step 5: Complete draft schedule, and put in a conference brochure format.	Ass't. Supt., Communication Dept.	Dec 18	Dec 22	
Step 6: Walk through with HS principal and HS tech staff for room assignments.	Ass't. Supt., HS principal, HS tech staff, Tech Director	Dec 19		Tech staff check for wireless capacity.
Step 7: Set up for online breakout session conference enrollment for staff.	Skyward staff set up online scheduling for staff	Dec 28	Jan 3	A school was created in Skyward, the student data management system, where teachers enrolled in their breakout sessions (Four plus one alternate).

(continued)

Task 1: Create a district-wide Big Cat Conference based on teaching staff Priority 1.

What Action Step Description	Who Person/ Dept. Responsible	When Begin Date	When Due Date	How Materials/ Resources Needed	How Much	Notes
Step 8: Review plans with principals and in the p.m. with PDC.	Ass't. Supt.; principals, PDC	Jan 2	Jan 2			Principals in conference center at 9:00a.m. PDC at 2:30p.m.
Step 9: Compose and send out district email with conference schedule and directions for enrolling in four session choices, plus one alternate; Staff enroll in choices.	Asst. Supt.; Communications Dept.; Skyward student data management staff	Jan 5	Jan 12			A school was created in Skyward, the student data management system where teachers enrolled in their breakout sessions (four plus one alternate).
Step 10: Schedules emailed to staff; Session Rosters emailed to staff facilitating the course.	Skyward staff;	Jan 12	Jan 14			Principals were asked to verify that all staff had their schedules & facilitators/ presenters had their rosters.

Step 11: Presenters/ facilitators prepare for class presentations; view room assignments/check out technologies & set up; tech staff do walk through on technology match to proposal.	Presenters/ facilitators; technology staff	Jan 12	Jan 16	

Figure 8.1 The Big Cat Conference

Figure 8.1 shows the district-wide staff development day Big Cat Conference brochure with several teacher breakout sessions.

(continued)

Task 1: Create a district-wide Big Cat Conference based on teaching staff Priority 1.

What Action Step Description	Who Person/ Dept. Responsible	When Begin Date	When Due Date	How Materials/ Resources Needed	How Much	Notes
Step 12: The Big Cat Conference Day: Welcomed by PDC; Attendance sheets distributed & collected to each classroom; PDC were hosts throughout the day.	District-wide licensed staff; food service; tech staff, three custodial staff	Jan 17	All Day Jan 17	Lunch-Three types of soup (chili, chicken tortilla, potato); Salad bar plus cold cuts— sliced meats/cheeses/ breads.	The Education Foundation	Celebration at the closing of the day with prize drawings, hot cocoa, popcorn, and ice cream sundaes party.
Step 13: Thank you notes—hand-written; then distributed through school mail with gift cards.	PDC, (gift cards: Partnerships with Walmart, Target, School Foundation)	Jan 22		7:30a.m. meeting.		Debriefing. Thank you note cards/envelopes printed & provided by district communications department.
Step 14: Session evaluations reviewed; data compiled and results shared with building principals.	PDC; Ass't. Supt.	Feb 3 Feb 10		PDC meetings both held after school.	$234 $234	Shared with their principals who recognized facilitators/session presenters at Feb faculty meetings.

Priority 1b: Organize and create graduate courses for credit taught by own staff/administrators to be held on school district campus.

Task 1: Staff will submit proposals to district administrative team who will partner with area colleges/universities, and teachers interested in graduate credit courses will pay for and enroll in courses created by district staff that meet the needs of staff based on survey results.

What Action Step Description	Who Person/Dept. Responsible	When Begin Date	When Due Date	How Materials/ Resources Needed	How Much	Notes
Step 1: Courses created based on data from online survey; draft course outlines with teaching possibilities listed.	PDC; Ass't. Supt.	Oct 3	Oct 30	Online Survey data—topics: curriculum design & instructional standards; instructional strategies; integration of technology into the teaching/ online resources.	$72	Cost to cover HS first block substitute.
	Principals	Oct 15	Oct 30			

(continued)

Task 1: Staff will submit proposals to district administrative team who will partner with area colleges/universities, and teachers interested in graduate credit courses will pay for and enroll in courses created by district staff that meet the needs of staff based on survey results.

What Action Step Description	Who Person/Dept. Responsible	When Begin Date	When Due Date	How Materials/ Resources Needed	How Much	Notes
Step 2: Proposals submitted to local colleges/ universities.	Ass't. Supt.	Nov 15	Dec 1			Ex: Teacher course focused on Science/ environmental projects at the Arkansas River for middle school students.
Step 3: Courses approved by colleges/ universities.	Newman Univ.; Southwestern College, FHSU, Friends Univ., WSU	Nov 30	Dec 30			Southwestern College, Newman Univ., FHSU.

Step	Who	Date	Date	Notes
Step 4: Courses to be offered to staff advertised/ enrollment forms available; Adjunct faculty for courses accepted.	All staff, PDC	Jan 5	Aug 31	Advertised through email, at staff meetings, PDC.
				Figure 8.2 shows an example from the Happy App-Y Classroom Course
Step 5: College Credit Courses/ workshops taught (e.g., Happy App-y Classroom; Guided Reading; Instructional Strategies that Work).	Staff who enrolled in college courses; Ass't. Supt.; Staff as Adjunct Faculty	Spring: Jan 20 Summer: Jun 7 Fall: Sept 8	May 14 July 28 Dec 9	

Figure 8.2 depicts the app name, icon, description, subject and standard(s) addressed, and district resource using the app from one class meeting.

(continued)

Priority 2: Staff will organize and create Summer Staff Academy workshops focused on the delivery and creation of general education interventions (GEIs) & instructional strategies that are evidence-based that will address a more student-centered approach to learning.

Task 1: Teachers interested in Summer Staff Academies will submit proposals to building principals to be reviewed by the PDC (to be verified by district administrative team that the work will help improve student learning outcomes).

What Action Step Description	Who Person/Dept. Responsible	When Begin Date	When Due Date	How Materials/ Resources Needed	How Much	Notes
Step 1: Creation of Summer Staff Academy guidelines and proposal forms for Summer Staff Academies; emailed to staff.	PDC; Ass't. Supt.	Mar 3 Mar 5	Mar 15	PDC meeting.	District costs for afternoon meetings: $234; morning meetings: $76	PDC pay for school meetings outside contract day.

Step 2: Proposal Deadline.	Available to all staff	April 2	April 9	
	Principals submit to Ass't. Supt.			
Step 3: Review and Approve Proposals.	PDC, Ass't. Supt.	April 11	Review proposals meeting.	$76	Substitute costs for high school reps.
Step 4: Notify principals and staff of accepted proposals.	PDC, Ass't. Supt.; principals, staff as facilitators	April 29			
Summer Staff Academies (e.g., Make it & Take it for student centers; create or revise common assessments;	Staff/facilitators meetings June 3-7	June 10-14	June 17-21	Met in various buildings & classrooms/common areas during the summer.	Approx. $3,375 per building.	Attendees $15 per hr/Facilitators $30 per hr.

(continued)

Task 1: Teachers interested in Summer Staff Academies will submit proposals to building principals to be reviewed by the PDC (to be verified by district administrative team that the work will help improve student learning outcomes).						
What Action Step Description	Who Person/Dept. Responsible	When Begin Date	When Due Date	How Materials/ Resources Needed	How Much	Notes
create outdoor science classroom projects; update & align grade level report cards to standards; vertical alignment of chapter books/novels per grade level; student fieldtrips aligned to curricular standards.	*Figure 8.3 Teachers collaborating during Summer Staff Academy*		*Figure 8.4 Teachers preparing student materials during Summer Staff Academy*		*Figure 8.5 Teachers completing math student packets during Summer Staff Academy*	

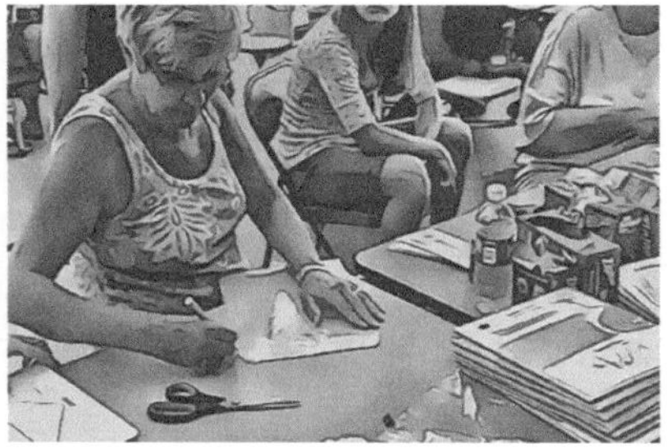

Figure 8.3 Teachers collaborating while creating standards-based report cards on computers during a Summer Staff Academy.

Figure 8.4 Teachers creating best practices, general education intervention student materials during a Summer Staff Academy.

Figure 8.5 Teachers preparing student packets with materials to improve math word problem solving—an evidence-based math strategy, FAST DRAW, during a Summer Staff Academy.

Action Plan	Jan 22	Jan 22	Feb 3	$1,350	Debriefing on Big Cat Conference.
Review Dates	Feb 3				Session Evaluations.
4. Destiny (The Playbook)	Aug 3-repeat AI 4-D cycle	Aug 3	Feb 9	All-day retreat.	Aug 3 Retreat-prepare for next school year.

The Playbook Scenario 4 AI summit was designed as a one-day event, with action plan commitments and meetings scheduled throughout the year. During the one-day AI summit, the PDC members and administrators were welcomed by the assistant superintendent, who was the AI facilitator. She asked that each person introduce themselves and share a positive, memorable event that happened in their school/classroom earlier in the week. There was an agenda overview for the day and an introduction to AI and the AI 4-D cycle.

Attendees participated in establishing team norms or ground rules. The process for establishing team norms or ground rules was much like the large group process with 120–130 participants (See Chapter 5). The 21 teachers and eight attending administrators were divided into four groups, where large chart paper was available at each table. They were asked to self-manage with one person as recorder, who took notes on the large chart paper, and one person as reporter, who would share what had been discussed to other table groups throughout the AI process. Each table brainstormed ground rules or team norms, where passing was an option. A countdown timer was used to keep groups on schedule. The reporter from each table group shared, then the lists were merged into one set of ground rules or team norms. They agreed to abide by the rules whenever meeting, to post the ground rules or team norms visually during meetings, and they agreed the rules could be revised at any time.

The 4-Ds

The discovery phase asked the four standard types of questions that are shared through storytelling, except in this scenario, the stories were captured via an online survey, with open-ended questions: (a) a high point or outstanding personal learning experience; (b) characteristics that made the learning experience effective, (c) list what participants valued in professional learning experiences; and (d) their wishes for the ideal, desired future for professional learning experiences. The discovery phase involved emails sent to the district's licensed staff requesting that they participate in the online survey over the course of three days.

The PDC and administrators reviewed the online survey results as part of their discovery phase on the day of the AI summit. Each table group, discussed the commonalities and themes, creating a list on large chart paper of the most effective professional development learning experience, the characteristics of the event, what was valued in the learning experience, and wishes for the ideal learning experience. The recorder at each table took notes and the reporters prepared what to share with another table group. The four table groups paired with another table group, so there were two table groups with

14 people in each group. Commonalities and themes were again identified, discussed, and determined and then shared with the whole group. The group then made comparisons and contrasts over the final two sets of lists. After analyzing the data and reviewing what the groups posted on large chart paper as common themes, the group could visually see what was valued by the district's licensed staff.

The dream phase asked for participants to take the best from the past or current situation and wishes from the discovery phase and imagine future possibilities for the ideal, preferred future. The group reviewed common themes from the discovery phase and in four table groups of seven people, they imagined what the ideal professional learning experiences could look like, considering the wishes for professional development from the online survey, listing 3–5 priorities on large chart paper. Each table group shared with another table group. They reviewed the data, highlighting or color-coding repeated phrases, identified common themes, and reviewed the data for characteristics valued from the discovery phase.

After discussion, the top 3–5 areas were prioritized with each person voting on ideas listed as most valued. Top priorities for wishes were shared with the whole group where common themes were discussed, and priorities were again determined, this time by voting with a set of three sticky dots. The top priorities were (a) Priority 1 was tied with the same number of votes so 1a) breakout sessions taught by teachers similar to attending a national conference, and 1b) create our own university graduate credit courses; (b) Priority 2: allow summer staff work, to become known as Summer Staff Academies, where teachers were paid in the summer to create, align curriculum for their classrooms; (c) Priority 3: Just in Time learning workshops; (d) Priority 4: hire staff as technology instructional coaches to help others with technology use and integration ideas; (e) Priority 5: arrange for early dismissal/late start days for additional collaboration time; and (f) Priorities 6 and 7: help provide financial aid to those who want to get their reading specialists or ESOL endorsements.

The design phase asked the participants to create bold, vision statements defining who they are and where they want the district to be bridging the discovery and dream phases. The bold, vision statements answered who they were and what the vision, purpose, and commitment to all staff entailed, so they could provide voice and act creating the ideal professional learning experiences for the district's preferred future.

The group was then asked to operationalize the bold, vision statements in the destiny phase by focusing on what it would take to make the vision statements happen. An action plan was created addressing each priority. The action plan included in the Playbook for Scenario 4 addresses the top three priorities, goals with tasks, and multiple action steps to be taken over the course of the next year. The tasks helped operationalize the priorities. Priority 1 was to simulate a national conference type professional learning day that included choice and control in learning topics through multiple break-out sessions where staff were teaching staff, so the task for Priority 1 was the creation of a district-wide Big Cat Conference (the school mascots were cats: lions, panthers, lynx, tigers, cubs, lionets, etc.). As noted in the action plan, Table 8.2, each task then had multiple action steps to accomplish the goal, so the desired, ideal professional learning experience became a reality. The PDC and administrators were asked to commit to the action plan, to make the dream happen, realizing the district's future. Before leaving the AI one-day summit, the group completed exit tickets and shared the most rewarding part of the day. They were overjoyed with the possibilities of making the dream happen, coming together as a district beginning with the district's upcoming staff development day.

Sustaining the plan

The AI facilitator, who was the assistant superintendent, held the PDC and building administrators accountable for the implementation of the action plans in the destiny phase, monitoring their progress toward a preferred future. The PDC and administrators committed to the action plans and completed the priorities voiced by staff, addressing the top six types of professional learning experiences within two years.

The first priority was to simulate a national conference with breakout sessions taught by staff and became known throughout the district as the Big Cat Conference, since all the mascots throughout the district were some type of cat—wildcat, panther, lynx, etc. The PDC and administrators met all action planning steps from creating breakout proposal forms and distributing the forms to advertising the Big Cat Conference in each building, soliciting between seven–ten proposals (60 or 120-minute workshops from their buildings) to coordinating the lunch on site and having staff drawings at the end of the day Big Cat Conference event. The PDC did a follow up with teachers who were presenters providing complimentary gift cards donated by area businesses and writing thank you notes.

The building administrators and PDC received graduate level course/workshop proposals from the teaching staff which were the first steps in addressing Priority 1b (Table 8.2). The PDC reviewed the proposals for criteria established in advancing student learning outcomes. The assistant superintendent for curriculum and instruction (as the AI facilitator) submitted several of the proposals to local colleges/universities, which proved to be successful such as the *Happy App-y Class* (Figure 8.2), where teachers of Prek-12 participated in addressing how technology apps could be used to help address student standards (both curricular and in areas of developing social/emotional learning skills). At this point in time, the district was blended in its approach using technologies, providing iPads to elementary students and Bring Your Own Device (BYOD) at the secondary levels or borrow school digital devices (e.g., iPads, Chromebooks, laptops) through the library check out system.

Priority 2 was a wish come true where teachers wanted to be paid in the summer to complete projects primarily focused on instructional strategies that were evidence-based, providing a more student-centered approach to learning. This was the beginning of the district's Summer Staff Academies. Building principals received staff development monies for teacher proposed summer staff academies held in their buildings to cover staff and material costs. Teaching staff were paid to attend and the teachers who facilitated the academies received double teacher pay. Summer staff academies varied with some lasting four hours or one-half day and others up to four days. Examples included (a) Make it & Take it for student centers, (b) create or revise common assessments grades 3–12, (c) create outdoor science classroom projects for grades 5–12, (d) update and align grade level report cards to new standards K-8, (e) vertical alignment of chapter books/novels per grade level, (f) K-6 student fieldtrips aligned to curricular standards, and (g) create standards - based report cards for summer school reading and math K-8. Figures 8.3, 8.4, and 8.5 represent some of the activities in the Summer Staff Academies.

The action plans for the destiny phase were completed with a celebration by the PDC and building administrators, then they repeated the AI process after receiving feedback from staff, session evaluations, and graduate level courses/workshops, and summer staff academy evaluations as they began the Year 2. As they planned the next year's staff development and in-service days, they chose to continue the Big Cat Conference each March. Graduate courses provided on campus that were created and taught by staff, and the summer staff academies also continued.

Now familiar with the AI 4-D cycle, the administrators are empowered for success, knowing they have a go-to change model and decision-making process that works. They were able to sustain and keep what was working, and then focused on how additional priorities could be met including Just in Time learning workshops designed to help with last minute needs such as entering grades in the student data management system; reallocating monies so several teachers could be half time technology integration specialists, instructional coaches, or strategists; working with administration on calendars dates and hours arranging for early dismissal/late start days for additional collaboration time throughout the district; and exploring options (e.g., prioritization of staff development monies, the education foundation) to provide financial aid to those who wanted to get their reading specialists, English as a Second Language (ESL) endorsements, or pursue a master's degree in special education.

Some of the greatest successes in leadership involve learning effective communication skills, development of shared leadership and collaborative decision-making skills, and inspiring a culture of empowerment; all were part of the AI 4-D process for administrators working with teachers within their buildings and district-wide to make the action plan happen, providing meaningful professional development for their staff. Chapter 9 provides an open playbook template, guiding questions to help you build the leadership capacity in your district or building, empowering them to use the AI 4-D cycle as the go-to change model.

9

Creating your own AI 4-D cycle playbook

The scenarios in Chapters 5–8 presented questions as the topic or focus of inquiry and showed how the appreciative inquiry (AI) 4-D cycle was used as the preferred decision-making process to bring rapid change and collaborative solutions while simultaneously focused on leadership development. The scenario samples addressed the following questions:

Chapter 5: *How can our school/district increase teacher retention at the elementary level?*
Chapter 6: *How can I help the administrative team build leadership capacity?* Or, specifically asks the building principal to look inward, reflecting on, *how does my leadership behavior support staff and influence student learning?*
Chapter 7: *How can our high school English department/PLC become a model teacher team productive and focused on improving student learning?*
Chapter 8: *How can our district inspire, encourage, and support classroom teachers through meaningful professional learning experiences?*

Chapter 9, Creating Your Own AI 4-D Cycle Playbook, provides the workspace and templates to guide your team through the AI process. To get started, think about the questions you have. When perusing conference session titles and descriptions for ASCD's recent national conferences, many questions or topics of concern were posed in the conference guide. The questions raised may be relevant topics for your school or district. A sampling of the questions included:

DOI: 10.4324/9781003350804-9

How can you "use the deeper learning approach to increase student engagement, address cultural awareness and diversity?" (McTighe & Sliver, 2022).

"How can we design learning spaces to support and engage modern students?" (Hayes Jacobs et al., 2021).

"How can you continue to build community in an online environment?" (Anderson & Pezzolla, 2021).

"How [do] culturally responsive school leaders develop culturally responsive schools"? (Gooden & Brooks-DeCosta, 2021).

"How do you recruit, develop, retain, and empower more male educators of color?" (Harris & Swimpson, 2021).

"How do we formulate effective feedback that empowers teachers to take charge of their professional learning and growth?" (Lawton & Simeral, 2022).

"How can we assure that learning leaders become the catalyst for school improvement that supports growth in each teacher and student?" (Cunningham-Morris & Pajardo, 2021).

"How do you create [inclusion] awareness in schools, thereby supporting safe and comfortable learning environments?" (Holik, 2021).

"How [can] a community unlock the full potential of all students through viable career and college pathways"? (Nova & Hall, 2021).

The questions posed by presenters may be similar to the ones you have in your educational setting. Answers to the questions are much easier when educational leaders have an inquiry process and change method that works, that is highly participatory where diverse voices are heard; one that allows creativity in imagining possibilities, and one that takes a positive approach versus one focused on problems. Once you begin to understand the AI process with its 4-D cycle as a decision-making change model, your school or district can build a future answering the questions that exist within your school community. The opportunity and possibilities are within reach and can be realized. Now is the time for you to act. Dream. Do.

A full-page advertisement was published on Monday, November 22, 2010, that appeared in the Wall Street Journal from NASDAQ OMX Group, Inc. It read:

> *Dream. Do.*
> *Two verbs too often separated.*
> *Dream without doing and your ideas wither on the vine.*
> *Do without dreaming and you bring nothing new to the world.*
> *But the moment dream and do come together, great things happen…*

Looking to take a dream as far as it will go?
Consider this your launch pad.

(p. R12)

Now it is your turn. Take the opportunity to Dream. Do. What questions or concerns do you and your team have that need to be addressed? Table 9.1 provides you with a template or workspace that guides you and your team through the AI 4-D change process. An action planning template, Table 9.2, is also provided to help develop the detailed steps and commitments needed to make the change happen. A sample timeline used to post possible action planning events along the wall is represented in Table 9.3. In addition, three different styles of agendas have been created for you to revise based on the size of group and time you and your team have available.

The AI 4-D cycle

Table 9.1 provides the template as a workspace to think through the development for your own AI event with the 4-D cycle.

Action plan

Table 9.2 The co-construction of the Action Plan template is a continuation of the destiny phase in the AI 4-D cycle where participants delineate the steps needed to make the dream happen. The action plan details the steps and addresses the who, what, when, where, how, and how much.

Agenda samples

Two-day agenda (for use with larger groups 50+ people)

Day 1 of 2
7:30–8:00 Continental Breakfast, Coffee, Tea, Soft Drinks
8:00–8:20 Welcome and Introductions
    Tables: Introduce self, where you work, how long you have worked for the district…or some type of icebreaker.

Table 9.1 Your playbook workspace: AI steps and questions for your topic/question

Steps	Description	Questions used to Guide the AI 4-D Cycle
Topic	Area of focus for change, innovation	How can…
Participants	Who needs to be involved in the change process?	People:
1. Discovery (Roles)	Part A: Share stories (the best from the past) to discover strengths, values, and wishes 1. A personal, past story.	1. Tell a personal, past story (related to the topic).
1. Discovery (Roles)	2. A high point experience.	2. Describe a high point experience with……(related to the topic).
		Where were you?
		Who was involved?
		What was happening?
1. Discovery (Roles)	3. What you value or characteristics that were valued about the experience.	3. List the qualities or characteristics that you valued…
		What do you value most about….?
1. Discovery (Roles)	4. List three wishes.	4. What three wishes do you have for…..
		1. 2. 3.

(*continued*)

Steps	Description	Questions used to Guide the AI 4-D Cycle
1. Discovery (Roles)	Part B: Identify the themes and determine what is most valued, best practices, strengths. • Review the data and highlight or color code repeated phrases or put in a spreadsheet.	List most common phrases on big chart paper; review the data for success factors discuss and vote on those most valued by the individuals. List the common themes: • • • • • • • •
1. Discovery (Roles)	• Post votes (e.g., three dots to each person or use a conference live voting system with clicker/ smartphones).	List the priorities (those with the most dots): 1. 2. 3. 4. 5.
2. Dream (Possible Plays)	Part A: Imagine future possibilities of what could be.	If the impossible were possible, what three wishes would you have so … (Consider the wishes stated in the Discovery phase).
		1. 2. 3.
2. Dream (Possible Plays)		Three years have passed, and the wishes have come true. You have returned to visit. What is happening? What are you seeing? What are people saying?

(continued)

Steps	Description	Questions used to Guide the AI 4-D Cycle
2. Dream (Possible Plays)	Part B: Identify the themes, and determine what is most valued, best practices, strengths.	Review the data and highlight or color code repeated phrases or put in a spreadsheet. List most common phrases on big chart paper; review the data for success factors, discuss and vote on those most valued by the individuals. List the common themes: • • • • • •
2. Dream (Possible Plays)	Post votes (e.g., three dots to each person or use a conference live voting system with clicker/ smartphones). Options for clarification are to review results through wish or dream statements (e.g. create a video, act out a skit, draw a mural or metaphor, write a story/poem, song) before writing vision statements.	List the top priorities (most votes/ dots): 1. 2. 3. 4. 5.

(continued)

Steps	Description	Questions used to Guide the AI 4-D Cycle
3. Design (Game Plan)	Create bold statements (vision statements) of an idealized future merging the best of what is valued from the discovery stage with the ideal future from the dream stage.	Take the best from 1b (Discovery) and 2b (Dream) to create the bold statements. In pairs begin to create the bold statements and share out to larger groups until consensus is reached. Ask, does the design use all the most important factors from the lists created in the discovery and dream phases?
	Prioritize and gain consensus of what should be and create the vision statement.	Address the four priority Ps: people (who we are and who we are when we are at our best); purpose (our goal), principles (what we value and believe), and practices (the world we want to live in and create together).
		Our vision:
		Our purpose:
		Our commitment to…..
		Review the bold, vision statements to ensure they are aligned with the priorities from 2b (Dream phase).
4. Destiny (The Playbook)	Create and commit to the action plan and to sustaining the plan, making it happen!	What will it take to make the dream come true? Create an action plan (see Table 9.2), a detailed plan outlining the steps to accomplish the goal(s) with an implementation timeline: address processes, people, resources that need to be in place, timelines, and celebration milestones. The action plan should answer the 4Ws + 2Hs:

(*continued*)

Steps	Description	Questions used to Guide the AI 4-D Cycle
		Who, What, Where, When, plus How, How much. • Write goals/SMART goals, decide on deadlines. • List the activities or tasks that need to be completed. • Create a visual so progress can be monitored and reviewed, reprioritized, etc. • Commit to the task or action you complete (List three ways you can help contribute to achieving the plan).

8:20–8:40 Overview of Topic, Purpose, and Intro to AI and 4-D Cycle

Topic: You have been invited to participate in a process that helps us answer the question, How can.....

Purpose: Our purpose is to answer the question, How can......by sharing stories and past experiences, imagining the possibilities, and collectively designing a plan that we co-construct to make our future, real through a process called the AI 4-D cycle.

Intro to AI & 4-D Cycle: The AI 4-D cycle has four stages or phases: Discovery, Dream, Design, and Destiny. The AI 4-D cycle is a change model focused on results; it is different from the traditional problem-solving models because the focus is on what works, what we value, what we envision for the future related to the topic—where we want to be at some point in time in relation to the topic or question asked today, how can...... Your participation is highly valued. Your engagement in today's activities, will lead to results. The group's collective decisions made today will shape our future.

8:40–9:00 Establishing Team Norms/Ground Rules

Tables: Each table creates a list of group norms/rules (e.g. limit side conversations, minimize cell phone/electronic usage). Self-manage determining the recorder and spokesperson for the table; next, partner with another table and share both table lists, then combine into one list. Repeat process until

Table 9.2 Is the action plan template

Destiny (The Playbook) Action Plan Topic: _____

Overall Objective:

Current Situation:

Priority 1:

Goal:

Task 1:

What Action Step Description	Who Person/Dept. Responsible	When Begin Date	When Due Date	How Materials/ Resources Needed	How Much	Notes
Step 1:						
Step 2:						
Step 3:						
Step 4:						

Action Plan Checkpoint Dates and Celebrations
Your Destiny,

Your Playbook!

Name of the Team Leader: (the person who is monitoring the progress of the action plan)

Contact Information:

Will communicate with each other via......

there are two overall lists in the room. Everyone returns to their table with the two lists posted and rules or norms are merged into one list. The final list is posted visually and reviewed for all to follow.

9:00–10:30 Discovery Phase-- Share stories (the best from the past) to discover strengths, values, and wishes.

9:00–9:25 In pairs, interview each other (Complete Worksheet 1—found after the Agenda samples in this chapter).

9:25–10:15 Share with table members what you heard from your partner in the paired interview.

10:15–10:30 Identify the themes and determine what is most valued, best practices, and strengths. Extract the highlights and key themes by answering the guiding questions collectively and post on large chart paper, then place on the wall.

10:30–10:45 Snack Break

10:45–11:45 Discovery Phase (Continued)

10:45–11:30 Paired tables share postings (e.g., Table 1 shares with Table 16). The two tables then note commonalities, identify the themes, and determine what is most valued, best practices, strengths, and wishes creating another set of lists with three–five items per list per question. The process is repeated with another group so overall the whole group has four sets of prioritized lists.

11:30–11:45 With four sets of lists posted on one wall, everyone is given a set of three sticky dots to place beside areas of most value by each person in the room. The dots now provide a visual representation showing what is valued by the whole group.

11:45–12:45 Lunch

12:45–1:00 Review the morning's Discovery phase & Introduce the Dream phase

1:00–2:45 Dream Phase-- Imagine future possibilities of what could be.

1:00–1:20 At table groups. In pairs complete (Worksheet 2).

1:20–2:00 Share with others in the table group.

Create a list of main points and themes with one person recording.

Consider the wishes from the Discovery phase.

Discuss and determine the top three–five points on one large chart paper sheet to share out with another table.

Post on wall with table number.

2:00–2:45 Paired tables share dream, imagined possibilities: (e.g., Table 1 shares with Table 8; Table 2 with Table 9, etc.). Compare and extract common points, themes. List most common phrases on big chart paper; review the data for success factors discuss and vote on those most valued by the individual, determining the top 3–5 points on one large chart paper sheet to share out with another table group.

Repeat process until there are four sets of dream sheets posted around the room.

Post votes (e.g., three dots to each person) or list on interactive board and vote with clickers or display using phones with live poll voting systems (e.g., Poll Everywhere, n.d.).

2:45–3:05 Snack Break

3:05–5:00 Dream Phase (Continued)

3:05–3:45 Return to original tables: Review results through wish or dream statements (e.g. create a video, act out a skit, draw a mural, metaphors, write a story/poem /song—this helps visualize and clarify meaning on the priorities from the lists) before writing vision statements.

3:45–5:00 Share creations or enactments.

Day 2 of 2

7:30–8:00 Continental Breakfast, Coffee, Tea, Soft Drinks

8:00–8:10 Welcome, Review Team Norms/Ground Rules (revise as needed)

8:10–8:20 Review Day 1 Accomplishments and Agenda for Day 2

8:20-10:15 Design Phase: Creating the Future

8:20–8:50 Table Groups: Create bold statements (vision statements) of an idealized future merging the best of what is valued from the discovery stage with the ideal future from the dream stage based on the visuals posted and the creations and enactments from the day before. Address the 4 Ps: people (who we are and who we are when we are at our best); purpose (our goal), principles (what we value and believe), and practices (the world we want to live in and create together). This includes our vision, purpose, and commitment along with other items listed that help define the preferred future.

8:50–9:30 Table group paired with another table group. Share bold, vision statements, analyze for commonalities, determine value of differences, prioritize and gain consensus.

9:30–10:15 Repeat the process until there are two sets of bold, vision statements. Discuss the final two sets of vision statements and then prioritize and gain consensus as a whole group.

10:15–10:35 Break (One person per table selected to review the two sets of vision statements and work together to determine and present one set of vision statements).

10:35–11:00 Design Phase: (Continue to Create the Future)

Whole Group: Return to original table groups. Presentation of the one set of vision statements; share and make adjustments as needed.

11:00–11:45 Destiny Phase: Create and commit to the action plan and to sustaining the plan, making it happen!

11:00–11:10 Introduction of priorities and action planning tasks.

11:10–11:45 Table groups each brainstorm what it would take to make the set of vision statements happen. Record and list on large chart paper. Discuss, prioritize, then sequence possible tasks and actions to be taken.

11:45–12:45 Lunch

12:45–4:30 Destiny Phase: (Continued, Making it Happen)

12:45–2:00 Share with another table group your top three–five priorities. Discuss, reflect on what actions should be taken, the sequencing, review for alignment with the set of vision statements. Create a second set of priorities, sequencing, tasks and actions that both table groups agree on.

2:00–2:40 Two members from each of the combined table groups post the top three priorities that are needed to make the vision statements happen and share with the whole group.

2:40–2:45 Each person, using sticky dots (three dots) votes on the top three actions/tasks to be taken as the highest priority they feel should be addressed to make the bold, vision statements happen.

2:45–3:05 Snack Break

3:05–4:00 Return to original table group: Determine what it would take to make Priority 1 happen—list the tasks and actions necessary; then address Priority 2 and Priority 3. Agree upon tasks and action items, then place on a large, long butcher paper rolled across one wall that serves as a timeline, placing the tasks and action items along the timeline. Table 9.3 is a sample timeline format.

Table 9.3 is a sample timeline format made from bulletin board paper and posted along the wall to help create an action planning timeline with the tasks and actions needed to make Priority 1 happen.

4:00–4:30 Individually, review the timelines, tasks, and actions. Make a personal commitment to at least one priority (forming action groups).

4:30–5:00 Closure.

4:30–4:40 Address how the priority action groups will be contacted after the meeting; address or reinforce what can be done immediately (to sustain the momentum and get the action going).

4:40–5:00 Individually: Complete exit ticket; share open microphone for comments and reflections.

One day agenda (for use with smaller groups <22 people)

Day 1 of 1

7:30–8:00 Continental Breakfast, Coffee, Tea, Soft Drinks

8:00–8:20 Welcome and Introductions

Table 9.3 A sample timeline format

Priority 1, Year 1:												
	Jan	Feb	Mar	April	May	June	July	Aug	Sept	Oct	Nov	Dec
What												
Who												
When												
Where												
How–Resources												
How much?												

Two tables with approximately ten people per table: Introduce self, where you work, how long you have worked for the district...and some type of icebreaker—(e.g. describe a funny or most memorable experience from your first year of teaching).

8:20–8:30 Overview of Topic, Purpose, and Intro to AI and 4-D Cycle—Narrative:

Topic: You have been invited to participate in a process that helps us answer the question, How can.....

Purpose: Our purpose is to answer the question, How can......by sharing stories and past experiences, imagining the possibilities, and collectively designing a plan that we co-construct to make our future, real through a process called the AI 4-D cycle.

Intro to AI & 4-D Cycle: The AI 4-D cycle has four stages or phases: Discovery, Dream, Design, and Destiny. The AI 4-D cycle is a change model focused on results; it is different from the traditional problem-solving models because the focus is on what works, what we value, what we envision for the future related to the topic—where we want to be at some point in time in relation to the topic or question asked today, How can......

Your participation is highly valued. Your engagement in today's activities, will lead to results. The group's collective decisions made today will shape our future.

8:30–8:50 Establishing Team Norms/Ground Rules

Tables: Each table creates a list of group norms/rules (e.g. limit side conversations, minimize cell phone/electronic usage). Self-manage determining the recorder and spokesperson for the table; next, partner with another table and share both table lists, then combine into one list. The final list is posted visually and reviewed for all to follow.

8:50–10:30 Discovery Phase-- Share stories (the best from the past) to discover strengths, values, and wishes.

8:50–9:10 In pairs, interview each other (Complete Worksheet 1—found after the agenda samples later in this chapter).

9:10–9:40 Share with table members what you heard from your partner in the paired interview.

9:40–10:00 Identify the themes and determine what is most valued, best practices, and strengths. Extract the highlights and key themes by answering the guiding questions collectively and post on large chart paper, then place on the wall.

10:00–10:30 Share postings with the other table. The two tables then note commonalities, identify the themes, and determine what is most valued, best practices, strengths, and wishes creating another set of lists with three–five items per list per question. With prioritized lists posted on one wall, everyone is given a set of three sticky dots to place beside areas of most value by each person in the room. The dots now provide a visual representation showing what is valued by the whole group.

10:30–10:45 Break

10:45–11:00 Introduce the Dream phase

11:00–11:45 Dream Phase-- Imagine future possibilities of what could be.

11:00–11:20 At table groups. In pairs complete (Worksheet 2).

11:20-11:45 Share with others in the table group.

Create a list of main points and themes with one person recording.

Consider the Wishes from the Discovery phase.

Discuss and determine the top three–five points on one large chart paper sheet to share out with another table.

Post on wall with table number.

11:45–12:45 Lunch

12:45–2:00 Dream Phase (Continued)-- Imagine future possibilities of what could be.

12:45–1:15 Each table shares dream, imagined possibilities. Compare and extract common points, themes. List most common phrases on big chart paper; review the data for success factors discuss and vote on those most valued by the individual, determining the top three–five points on one large chart paper sheet to share out with another table group. Post votes (e.g. three dots to each person or list on interactive board and vote with clicker vote or vote and display using live voting poll systems such as Poll Every-where (n.d.).

1:15–1:45 Back to original tables: Review results through wish or dream statements (e.g. create a video, act out a skit, draw a mural, metaphors, write a story/poem, song—this helps visualize and clarify meaning on the priori-ties from the lists) before writing vision statements.

1:45–2:30 Share creations or enactments.

2:30–2:45 Snack Break

2:45–3:30 Design Phase: Creating the Future

2:45–3:30 Table Groups: Create bold statements (vision statements) of an idealized future merging the best of what is valued from the discovery stage with the ideal future from the dream stage based on the visuals posted and the creations and enactments from the day before. Address the 4 Ps: people (who we are and who we are when we are at our best); purpose (our goal), principles (what we value and believe), and practices (the world we want to live in and create together). This includes our vision, purpose, and commit-ment along with other items listed that help define the preferred future.

Share with the other table group. Share bold, vision statements, analyze for commonalities, determine value of differences, prioritize and gain consensus. Discuss the final two sets of vision statements and then work together to determine one set of vision statements.

3:30–4:45 Destiny Phase: Create and commit to the action plan and to sustaining the plan, making it happen!

3:30–3:40 Introduction of priorities and action planning tasks.

3:40–4:00 Table groups each brainstorm what it would take to make the set of vision statements happen. Record and list on large chart paper. Discuss, prioritize, then sequence possible tasks and actions to be taken.

4:00–4:45 Share with the other table group your group's top three–five priorities. Discuss, reflect on what actions should be taken, the sequencing, review for alignment with the set of vision statements. Create a second set of priorities, sequencing, tasks and actions that both table groups agree on to make the bold, vision statements happen. Determine what it would take to make Priority 1 happen—list the tasks and actions necessary; then address Priority 2 and Priority 3. Agree upon tasks and action items, then place on a large, long butcher paper rolled across one wall that serves as a timeline, placing the tasks and action items along the timeline (Table 9.3).

Individually, review the timelines, tasks, and actions. Make a personal commitment to at least one priority. List three ways you could continue your involvement with the action plan.

4:45–5:00 Closure

Address who the team leader will be and how participants will be contacted; address or reinforce what can be done immediately (to sustain the momentum and get the action going).

Individually: Complete exit ticket; share open microphone for comments and reflections.

Agenda for three one-hour meetings (for use with 2–16 participants)

The team leader/meeting facilitator will have….

Prepared worksheet questions for the topic/question to be addressed.

Communicated with participants in advance of the meeting.

Emailed the agenda and purpose, Worksheet 1, any materials/resources needed related to the topic.

Set up the meeting room and provided large chart paper, markers, and sticky dots.

In advance of the meeting, participants will have…

Read the agenda with topic/question and purpose.

Completed Worksheet 1 (if a new topic/question is being addressed).

Brought materials and resources as requested.

Meeting 1 of 3
8:00–8:05 Overview of Topic, Purpose, Review Team Norms/Ground Rules
8:05–8:20 Discovery: Randomly pair participants and share the completed Worksheet 1.

8:20–8:50 Discovery: Share with table group what the other person shared and vice versa.

8:50–9:00 Discovery: Analyze what was shared and create lists with common themes---past, personal experience related to the topic; high point experience; what is valued/characteristics; three wishes.

Meeting 2 of 3
8:00–8:20 Dream Phase: Complete the dream (Worksheet 2) in pairs and share the dreams, imagined possibilities. Review the wishes from the discovery phase. Compare and extract common points, themes. List most common phrases on big chart paper; review the data for success factors, discuss, and vote on those most valued individually, determining the top 3–5 points on one large chart paper sheet.

Optional (Add as another meeting). Review prioritized results through wish or dream statements (e.g. create a video, act out a skit, draw a mural, metaphors, write a story/poem, song—this helps visualize and clarify meaning on the priorities from the lists) before writing vision statements.
8:20–8:40 Design Phase: Creating the Future
Create bold statements (vision statements) of an idealized future merging the best of what is valued from the discovery stage with the ideal future from the dream stage based on the visuals posted and the creations and enactments from the day before. Address the four priority Ps: people (who we are and who we are when we are at our best); purpose (our goal), principles (what we value and believe), and practices (the world we want to live in and create together). This includes our vision, purpose, and commitment along with other items listed that help define the preferred future.

Share with the other table group. Share bold, vision statements, analyze for commonalities, determine value of differences, prioritize and gain consensus. Discuss the final two sets of vision statements and then work together to determine one set of vision statements.
8:40–9:00 Destiny Phase: Create and commit to the action plan and to sustaining the plan, making it happen!
Table groups each brainstorm what it would take to make the set of vision statements happen. Record and list on large chart paper. Discuss, prioritize, then sequence possible tasks and actions to be taken.

Share with the other table group your group's top three–five priorities. Discuss, reflect on what actions should be taken, the sequencing, review for alignment with the set of vision statements. Agree on priorities, sequencing, tasks, and actions that both table groups agree on to make the bold, vision statements happen. Place on the posted timeline (Table 9.3) and then complete the action plan form.

Meeting 3 of 3
8:00–8:30 Destiny: Review the co-constructed action plan, revise as needed. Commit to the plan. List three ways you can help contribute to achieving the plan—the desired future for your team, school, or district.
8:30–9:00 Begin your journey to a desired future...destiny.

Participant worksheets

Discovery phase: worksheet 1
Take the next five minutes to jot down notes to the following questions. In pairs, your partner will interview you and take notes as you share your stories. Then, you will reverse roles and your partner will share stories as you listen and take notes.

Tell a personal, past story (related to the topic).
Describe a high point experience with......(related to the topic).
Where were you?
Who was involved?
What was happening?
What do you value most about....?
What three wishes do you have for.....?

1.
2.
3.

Note: When finished, join your small group table of eight–ten people.

Dream phase: worksheet 2
Review the wishes from Worksheet 1.
If the impossible were possible, what three wishes would you have......
Three years have passed. Your wishes have come true! What are you seeing and what are they doing and saying?

Design phase: worksheet 3

Create bold, vision statements based on the top three priorities. Address the 4 Ps: people (who we are and who we are when we are at our best); purpose (our goal), principles (what we value and believe), and practices (the world we want to live in and create together). This includes our vision, purpose, and commitment along with other items listed that help define the preferred future.

Our vision….
Our purpose….
Our commitment….

Destiny phase: worksheet 4

What will it take to make the dream come true?

Create action plans to address the bold, vision statements. Include goals, tasks, and action steps.

How will you personally contribute to making the dream happen, become the preferred future?

List three ways you can continue the momentum, be involved, and/or promote the action plan.

1.
2.
3.

Exit ticket

Tell the most impressive story or comment made throughout this process over the past two days that you want to remember and want others to know/remember.

What are you most excited about going forward?

Summary: Chapter 9 creating your own AI 4-D cycle playbook

The templates with guiding questions for the 4-D cycle have been provided for you to plan out your first AI meeting or summit. A variety of agendas have been created based on the size of your group and the time available (a two-day agenda, a one-day agenda, and an agenda for three one-hour meetings for limited meetings such as early-late starts or job-embedded staff development times. The worksheets and exit tickets have been provided. There is a saying, "the more, the more". The more you practice, the better you become at using the AI process to help bring about change.

Change is a constant and approaching it with a solutions-based process that involves all team members and uses strengths-based language in resolving situations was priority for writing this book. Among Whitaker's (2013) list of what great teachers do is that they "create a positive atmosphere in their classrooms and schools" (p. 123). We, as educational leaders, must do the same for our district and building level administrative teams; we must provide opportunities for administrators to intentionally practice leading, becoming shared decision-makers.

The preferred practice in addressing change is through the AI 4-D cycle where all are encouraged to participate, where collaboration is valued, and change occurs in an "appreciative", positive atmosphere. The goal was to help bring clarity to you and your team as you confront the day-to-day challenges or problems of practice like the questions asked at ASCD's national conferences. This book was written for educational leaders (e.g., principals, superintendents, boards of education, scholars in educational administration, education service centers, state agencies, learning organizations, organization development theorists, etc.) interested in building a cohesive educational community with a proven change method, AI with its 4-D cycle. How you address change, must become intentional and routine. Now it is time for you to coach—Dream. Do.

References

Anderson, M., & Pezzolla, K. (2021). *Through the lens of COVID: Continuing to build classroom culture online for effective, equitable instruction* [Conference session 1140]. ASCD Annual Conference-Empowered and Connected, Virtual eShow. https://s7.goeshow.com/ascd/empower/2021/conference_program_sessions.cfm

Cunningham-Morris, A., & Pajardo, P. (2021). *The principal influence: Developing leadership capacity in principals and aspiring principals* [Conference Session 1137]. ASCD Annual Conference-Empowered and Connected, Virtual eShow. https://s7.goeshow.com/ascd/empower/2021/conference_program_sessions.cfm

Gooden, M. A., & Brooks-DeCosta, D. (2021). *How culturally responsive school leaders can develop culturally responsive schools* [Conference session 1116]. ASCD Annual Conference-Empowered and Connected, Virtual eShow. https://s7.goeshow.com/ascd/empower/2021/conference_program_sessions.cfm

Harris, D., & Swimpson, I. (2021). *How do you recruit, develop, retain, and empower more male educators of color?!: You bond* [Conference Session 1117]. ASCD Annual Conference-Empowered and Connected, Virtual eShow. https://s7.goeshow.com/ascd/empower/2021/conference_program_sessions.cfm

Hayes Jacobs, H., Nair, P., & Alcock, M. (2021, June 23–25). *Designing learning spaces to support and engage modern students* [Conference Session 1107]. ASCD Annual Conference-Empowered and Connected, Virtual eShow. https://s7.goeshow.com/ascd/empower/2021/conference_program_sessions.cfm

Holik, M. (2021). *Creating awareness creates inclusive and equitable classrooms: Advocate, don't witness* [Conference Session 1210]. ASCD Annual Conference-Empowered and Connected, Virtual eShow. https://s7.goeshow.com/ascd/empower/2021/conference_program_sessions.cfm

Lawton, D. & Simeral, A. (2022). Formulating effective feedback: Changing teacher practice one conversation at a time. [Conference Session 5656A]. ASCD Annual Conference. https://s7.goeshow.com/ascd/annual/2022/conference_program_sessions.cfm

McTighe, J., & Silver, H. (2022). *Teaching for deeper learning.* [Conference Session PC06]. ASCD Annual Conference. https://s7.goeshow.com/ascd/annual/2022/conference_program_sessions.cfm

NASDAQ OMX Group, Inc. (2010). Dream. Do. *The Wall Street Journal.* R12. https://www.wsj.com/

Nova, B. & Hall, J. (2021). *It is possible! How a community can unlock the full potential of all students through viable career and college pathways* [Conference Session 1221]. ASCD Annual Conference-Empowered and Connected, Virtual eShow. https://s7.goeshow.com/ascd/empower/2021/conference_program_sessions.cfm

Poll Everywhere. (n.d.). *Instant poll voting on smartphones.* Retrieved August 13, 2022, from https://www.polleverywhere.com/smartphone-web-voting.

Whitaker, T. (2013). *What great teachers do differently: 17 things that matter most (2nd ed).* Routledge.

Epilogue

Most often the "how" to do something is left out of the details. Knowing that the foundation for a better future lies with the familiarity of the appreciative inquiry (AI) process as a framework in resolving and understanding the possibilities is a given. With AI, any challenge can be approached with confidence. What can you do to ensure success within your team? I urge you to practice the AI process, so you too, can bring clarity to how change can happen within your school or district.

As a former English and math teacher, a building level school administrator, and a district level assistant superintendent, I have found AI to be the most valuable group facilitation tool and approach to help bring about change in a rapid manner that is collaborative and inclusive. I continue to use AI with graduate students, especially encouraging peer coaching triads with teachers new to special education. I love working with content specific teacher departments, grade level teacher teams, professional learning communities, and developing district administrative teams, focused on the intentionality of implementing AI as their preferred choice for making change happen. I work confidently, knowing that AI is an effective and efficient process whether in small or large group settings.

The questioning techniques are framed within a positive context to promote and encourage interactive dialogue. The discovery process allows group time to reflect on past experiences and become familiar with the history of the situation, which helps provide the transition needed to look at possibilities for any situation and from diverse voices. Every time I use the AI change model, the group becomes more energized and engaged to the point that they then become consumed in where they want to go with their goals and priorities. Their newly acquired knowledge or application of such becomes their focus, their destiny. The change model process, the action plan, and the commitment levels are guided by the participants and their creative work. The power of AI is in helping educational leaders understand that they have the capacity to change and in a positive way, where they have a choice in participating, to be involved, and to be heard. I believe AI and the 4-D cycle is the most important tool an educational leader can have, as it is the vehicle for change. Becoming familiar with AI and the 4-D change model empowers you for success.

Index

For Product Safety Concerns and Information please contact our
EU representative GPSR@taylorandfrancis.com Taylor & Francis
Verlag GmbH, Kaufingerstraße 24, 80331 München, Germany